American Horticultural Society

75 GREAT AMERICAN GARDEN PLANTS

William E. Barrick

Oxmoor House®

To my wife, Jessica,
for her continued love, support,
and encouragement.

Library of Congress Catalog Number: 97-75804
ISBN: 0-8487-1620-5
Manufactured in the United States of America
First Printing 1998

Editor-in-Chief: Nancy Fitzpatrick Wyatt
Senior Homes Editor: Mary Kay Culpepper
Senior Editor, Editorial Services:
    Olivia Kindig Wells
Art Director: James Boone

75 Great American Garden Plants

Editor: Ann Marie Harvey
Copy Editor: Anne S. Dickson
Editorial Assistant: Allison Ingram
Associate Art Director: Cynthia R. Cooper
Designer: Larry Hunter
Production Director: Phillip Lee
Associate Production Manager:
    Vanessa Cobbs Richardson
Production Assistant: Faye Porter Bonner

We're Here for You!
We at Oxmoor House are dedicated to
serving you with reliable information that
expands your imagination and enriches
your life. We welcome your comments and
suggestions. Please write us at:

Oxmoor House, Inc.
Editor, *75 Great American Garden Plants*
2100 Lakeshore Drive
Birmingham, AL 35209

To order additional publications,
call 1-205-877-6560.

About the Author

Dr. William E. Barrick is executive vice
president and director of gardens at Callaway
Gardens in Pine Mountain, Georgia. Born in
Dothan, Alabama, Barrick received both a
bachelor's degree in botany and a master of
science degree in ornamental horticulture from
Auburn University, and a Ph.D. in landscape
horticulture from Michigan State University.
Dr. Barrick is current chairman of the
American Horticultural Society, past president
of the American Association of Botanical
Gardens and Arboreta, and winner of the
Arthur Hoyt Scott Medal. He is also a member
of the Auburn University Agricultural Council,
Georgia Conservancy, and the National
Wildflower Research Center Board.

Photography Credits

Suzanne Bales: 9, 115, 117, 138, 157
William E. Barrick: 13, 17, 44, 53, 63, 79, 87, 101, 120-121, 125, 135
Van Chaplin: back cover, 3, 9, 11, 20-21, 24-25, 28, 33, 38-39, 60, 69-70, 74, 83, 90-91, 102, 106, 108-109, 112, 124, 137, 145, 152-153
Gary Clark: 54-55
Tina Evans Cornett: 103
Mike Dirr: 12, 31, 35-36, 48, 57, 62, 66-67, 75, 80, 82, 84-86, 88-89, 118-119
Derek Fell: 3, 16, 19, 22-23, 27, 36, 50, 68, 72, 92, 126-127, 131, 140-141
Mary-Gray Hunter: 105, 136
Dency Kane: 26, 51, 73, 116, 130, 143
Larry LeFever from Grant Heilman: 41, 81
Chris Little: 14-15, 18, 30, 37, 45, 64-65, 100, 133, 156
Sylvia Martin: back cover, 29, 46-47, 97, 111, 148, 151, 154-155
Beth Maynor: back cover, 56, 61, 99, 110, 114, 134
Mary Carolyn Pindar: 132, 149
Rannels from Grant Heilman: 93
Allen Rokach: 144
Runk/Schoenberger from Grant Heilman: 40

Contents

Black tupelo, page 18

Bottlebrush buckeye, page 28

Leadwort, page 92

Cover Photographs

Front Cover: Southern magnolia (p.122)

Back Cover (from left): Loquat (p.98), Woodland phlox (p.154), Oakleaf hydrangea (p.106), Japanese pieris (p.82), Chinese pistachio (p.48), Bluestar (p.24), Flowering dogwood (p.60), Mexican bush sage (p.100), American beautyberry (p.10)

Celebrate 75 Great Years with the American Horticultural Society

The American Horticultural Society (AHS) was founded in 1922 as an educational, non-profit organization to recognize and advance excellence in American horticulture. Today, AHS strives to educate America's gardeners to appreciate, understand, and promote the beauty and environmental contribution that plants and gardens bring to people's lives.

The Diamond Jubilee

In 1997, AHS celebrated its 75th anniversary with a year-long calendar of 75 nationwide horticultural activities, including flower shows, county fairs, and educational programs.

River Farm

This book also celebrates the anniversary of AHS. A committee of AHS members nominated more than 200 garden plants to be considered for inclusion in the book. Then a group of horticulturists chose the top 25 perennials, trees, and shrubs that are profiled in the following pages.

The American Horticultural Society headquarters is in Alexandria, Virginia, at River Farm, which was once a working farm owned by George Washington. From the headquarters building, visitors can view the Potomac River and 25 acres of gardens, including an azalea garden, a national trial garden site of the American Dahlia Society, extensive perennial gardens, and a children's garden.

Teaching America's Gardeners

The AHS accomplishes its mission through its outreach programs, such as the National Youth Gardening Symposium. This program brings together teachers, public garden educators, and interested adults to show children how to appreciate the joy and value of gardening. Another program, the Gardeners' Information Service, is a toll-free hotline and E-mail service staffed by volunteers that provides members with up-to-date gardening information. Internships provide hands-on experience for horticulture students to earn academic credit while working at River Farm. A travel program gives members access to the finest gardens in the United States and abroad. And through its awards program, AHS salutes individuals, organizations, and institutions that make significant contributions to American horticulture.

The Benefits of Membership

AHS members represent all 50 states, the District of Columbia, and many foreign countries. Membership is open to anyone with an interest in gardening. Members receive a full-color, bimonthly publication, *The American Gardener*, which includes in-depth gardening information in feature articles, news, book reviews, and a calendar of nationwide horticultural events. Free admission to more than 120 North American public gardens, conservatories, and arboreta is also included, as well as free passes to flower shows and home and garden shows. Access the AHS Web site at http://www.ahs.org or call 1-800-777-7931 for more information.

What Is a Great American Garden Plant?

Although no two gardeners agree on what makes a great American garden plant, most want dependable, easy-to-care-for plants. Gardeners also demand plants that resist pests and diseases and adapt to a variety of soil types and water conditions. Favorite plants are often linked to childhood memories of gardens created by family members or neighbors. Nearly half of the plants in the book are native to the United States, and both deciduous and evergreen trees and shrubs represented. The majority of plants grow well over a wide range of hardiness zones. Only a few are restricted to frost-free regions of the United States.

Plant Groups

Trees form the backbone of a garden. More than any other type of plant, trees define a sense of place and bring human scale to urban and residential gardens. These towering plants invoke a sense of awe and wonder, from the grandeur and tenacity of dawn redwood (page 56) to the grace and serenity of live oak (page 96). Most of us have fond childhood memories of climbing trees or flying high from swings anchored to sturdy branches. Trees vividly sig-

Mountain Laurel, page 102

nal the changing seasons, from the dramatic fall color of New England maples and oaks, to the clouds of white dogwood flowers unfolding in Southern gardens. Trees can be landmarks, too, distinguishing a site with their beauty. Southern magnolia (page 122), featured on the cover of this book, is considered by many horticulturists to be the ultimate broad-leafed, evergreen ornamental plant.

Shrubs define the middle layer in the garden. With proper selection, these plants can provide color in the garden throughout the year. Shrubs herald spring, brighten the blue skies of summer, and supply a colorful spectacle in fall in shades of yellow, orange, and red foliage. They even spark gray winter days with colorful fruit. There are many species and selections to choose from for each climate zone. Shrubs are the workhorses of most gardens. They screen undesirable views, serve as backgrounds for annuals and perennials, and prevent erosion by stabilizing the soil on steep slopes.

Perennials bring an array of color, texture, and fragrance to the garden, year after year. From the first crocuses emerging through snow cover, to bright bouquets of threadleaf coreopsis (page 138), to the last gasp of color of stonecrop (page 128), carefully planned perennials are rewarding throughout the growing season.

Red Maple, page 111

Spanish Bluebells, page 124

How to Plant

Whether you are planting a tree, a shrub, or a perennial, it is essential to prepare the soil properly to ensure success.

The first step is to have a soil sample analyzed at the local agricultural Extension service. The results of these tests will determine the degree of soil acidity, alkalinity, type, and fertility level.

For trees and shrubs, the soil should be loose and fertile in order for the roots to expand fully. Additions of organic matter, such as compost, sphagnum peat moss, or rotted manure, improve nutrients and moisture retention.

When planting trees or shrubs, dig a hole at least two to three times the width of the root ball and only slightly deeper. When planting containerized plants, use a shovel to slice the sides of the root ball to make it easier for the roots to grow into the newly prepared soil. After backfilling soil around the root ball, tamp the soil to remove air pockets. Make sure to plant balled-and-burlapped or containerized plants at the same depth that they grew, or slightly higher, since settling can occur after watering. Water the plant thoroughly to settle the soil around the roots and to remove air pockets. Finally, apply 2 to 3 inches of mulch around the perimeter of the planting area.

You can plant perennials as either bare-root plants or as container plants. Bare-root perennials should be planted while they are still dormant. Most nurseries time their digging to coincide with the proper planting stage for the region. Soak bare roots in water before planting. Timing is not as critical with containerized perennials, but most should be planted in late fall or early spring. Soil preparation is as important with perennials as with trees and shrubs. To ensure success, follow the same procedures to test, prepare, and amend the soil.

Plant Hardiness Zone Map

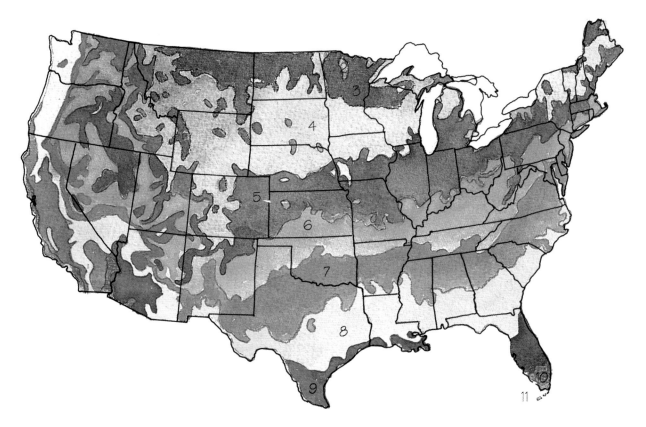

T he United States Department of Agriculture (USDA) has charted low temperatures throughout the country to determine the ranges of average low readings. The map above is based loosely on the USDA Plant Hardiness Zone map, which was drawn from these findings. It does not take into account heat, soil, or moisture extremes and is intended as a guide, not a guarantee. The zones on this map are referred to throughout the book.

	Zone 2	-50	to	-40°F
	Zone 3	-40	to	-30°F
	Zone 4	-30	to	-20°F
	Zone 5	-20	to	-10°F
	Zone 6	-10	to	0°F
	Zone 7	0	to	10°F
	Zone 8	10	to	20°F
	Zone 9	20	to	30°F
	Zone 10	30	to	40°F
	Zone 11		above	40°F

African Lily

Agapanthus africanus

The vibrant blooms of African lily bring contrast to the summer garden, especially when paired with yellow or other bright-colored flowers. Often called Lily-of-the-Nile, this perennial is popular among florists for its height and elegant appearance. It produces clusters of deep blue flowers in May and June on stems reaching as tall as 20 inches.

In the Landscape

Plant African lily in Zones 8 to 11. It doesn't grow well in colder climates. In the Gulf Coast states and California, African lily is often used as a ground cover by planting large numbers together.

In cooler climates, African lily is best grown as a greenhouse or container plant. After it flowers, the amount of water the plant receives should be reduced and the crown (where the plant's top growth originates) should be allowed to dry out. As spring approaches, the plant should be watered again to force new growth.

Planting and Care

African lily spreads by underground rhizomes (stems that grow at the soil surface). Plant this perennial in well-drained, fertile soil in partial shade or full sun. Although African lily blooms best when slightly crowded, plants should be divided every three to four years. During the growing season, adequate watering is

Plant African lily rhizomes 1 inch deep and 1½ feet apart in sunny beds, borders, or containers.

important to prevent the fleshy roots from drying out.

Species and Selections

There are many named selections of African lily with varying shades of blue flowers.

For more cold-hardy plants, try the popular Headbourne hybrids.

Other selections that grow well in Zone 8 differ only in flower color. 'Albus' produces white flowers, while 'Loch Hope' has the truest blue flowers. A related species, Oriental agapanthus (*A. orientalis*), has softer, more refined leaves. Its flower spike blooms profusely, bearing 40 to 100 blue flowers.

AT A GLANCE

Plant type: perennial

Features: clusters of funnel-shaped flowers in May and June on tall, thick stems

Colors: blue or white blooms

Height: foliage to 20 inches, flower stalk to 3 to 4 feet

Light: full sun to partial shade

Soil: well drained, fertile

Water: medium during summer, low during winter

Problems: none specific

Native: Africa

Range: Zones 8 to 11

Remarks: doesn't require staking; many selections varying in flower color and height

American Beautyberry

Callicarpa americana

During late September and into October, the dazzling magenta-colored berries of American beautyberry burst forth with color in the garden. When brought indoors, the berries can become a striking addition to a floral arrangement.

Best known in the Southeastern United States for its unusual-colored fruit, American beautyberry flourishes in the woodlands of Virginia to Florida and west to Texas.

In the Landscape

This shrub is a large, sprawling plant, growing as tall as 8 feet and equally wide. It is most at home in a woodland or natural setting, where it has plenty of room to spread. Its branches grow in a lanky, unkempt habit, and its coarse foliage is dull, yellow-green. In the summer, hidden among the branches are pale pink blooms, which give way to the plant's magenta-colored fall berries.

Planting and Care

For abundant fruit, plant American beautyberry in full sunlight or light shade. Choose a spot with moist, well-drained soil. Once established, this shrub is more tolerant of poorer soil conditions and drought. To highlight the berries, plant this shrub in front of a dark wall or in front of evergreen plants. Prune American beautyberry to the ground in late winter if the shrub becomes overgrown.

American beautyberry provides a natural-looking screen along a property line (above). The magenta berries give the shrub its name (right).

Species and Selections

'Lactea', a selection with white berries, contrasts well with the magenta-colored species. It also attracts more birds.

Purple beautyberry (*C. dichotoma*), a native of China and Japan, combines all the attributes of American beautyberry on a smaller shrub. The light pinkish lavender berries are also smaller.

Japanese beautyberry, *C. japonica*, has violet to metallic purple fruit. It is a hardier plant, and grows well in Zones 5 to 8.

Bodinier beautyberry, *C. bodinieri*, a species that grows well in Zones 5 and 6, produces lavender-blue colored fruit. It flowers and fruits best if several plants are grown together.

AT A GLANCE

Plant type: deciduous shrub

Features: magenta-colored fall berries, sprawling form

Colors: pale pink flowers

Height: 5 to 8 feet

Light: full sun to partial shade

Soil: slightly moist

Water: medium

Problems: none specific

Native: Southeastern United States

Range: Zones 7 to 10

Remarks: berry-laden branches useful in floral decorations

American Hop Hornbeam

Ostrya virginiana

American hop hornbeam gets its name from the resemblance its fruit have to the beer-flavoring hops. Also called ironwood, this graceful native tree has dense, durable wood and rough, scaly bark. Because of its resilience, the wood is often used for fence posts, tool handles, and mallets.

In the Landscape

Although it grows slowly, this medium-sized shade tree reaches a mature height of 25 to 40 feet, with a spread of 15 to 25 feet in about 10 to 15 years. American hop hornbeam can be a multitrunked tree or a single-trunked tree. Because it tolerates poor soil, it is a good choice for urban settings.

In early summer, the tree sports light green fruit pods that hang in abundant clusters. The pods turn brown, remaining on the branches for several months.

In some years, the leaves turn yellow in October and are colorful for a short period of time. The tree is deciduous, shedding its leaves each fall. Its twigs and branches are so tough that they are rarely damaged by wind.

Plant American hop hornbeam as a lawn, park, or golf course tree. This plant also grows well in narrow spaces.

Planting and Care

American hop hornbeam transplants well from containers. Since it is an understory tree

A row of American hop hornbeam provides graceful structure to the landscape (right). The pale green fruit pods appear in September (above).

that grows in the shadow of larger trees, it will flourish in partial shade or full sun.

American hop hornbeam tolerates a wide range of soil, from clay to loam to sandy soil, as long as it has good drainage. This tree requires little maintenance and is usually pest- and insect-free.

Species and Selections

A member of the birch family, American hop hornbeam is related to river birch (page 112), *Betula nigra*. Two other species that have similar characteristics, European hornbeam (*O. carpinifolia*) and Japanese hornbeam (*O. japonica*), are also available.

AT A GLANCE

Plant type: deciduous tree

Features: light green fruit pods; dense, durable wood; shaggy bark

Height: 25 to 40 feet

Light: full sun to partial shade

Soil: well drained

Water: medium

Problems: none specific

Native: North America

Range: Zones 3 to 9

Remarks: can be grown as single-trunked or multi-trunked tree

Bald Cypress

Taxodium distichum

Bald cypress is a native of Southern swamps, but this deciduous tree adapts so well to different horticultural conditions, it is just as much at home growing in an urban setting. Bald cypress is not a true cypress, but is a member of the same family as the redwoods. Its timber is often used in boats and greenhouses because it resists decay.

Soft, needlelike leaves give bald cypress a fine texture (above). Plant several trees together to add height to the landscape (right).

In the Landscape

Bald cypress grows quickly into a neat cone shape. Mature trees can reach a height of 50 to 70 feet with a spread of 20 to 30 feet. Its fine-textured, dark green needles are light green in spring and change to gray-green in late summer. The needles turn russet brown in autumn, before falling to form a soft carpet of natural mulch under the canopy.

The tree's trunk is broad, almost buttressed, particularly when grown near water. In the swamps, bald cypress forms a wide trunk base and above-ground roots, called "knees."

Planting and Care

To reach its full form, bald cypress should be grown in full sun, but it will accept a great deal of shade.

Bald cypress prefers moist, rich soil, although it tolerates poor, dry soil. Plant it in soil where the pH is slightly acidic, or the foliage will turn an anemic yellow. To avoid this, use an acid-forming fertilizer.

You can easily transplant bald cypress as a balled-and-burlapped tree or a small container tree. The species is maintenance free, but it occasionally suffers from spider mites and bagworms. Treat these pests with insecticide sprays.

Species and Selections

A few selections are known for their lacy, fernlike foliage and graceful, loose form.

'Monarch of Illinois' has a wide-spreading form, while 'Pendens' has distinct drooping branches. 'Shawnee Brave' has a narrow, cone-shaped growth habit. A related plant, pond cypress (*T. ascendens*), has a more columnar shape than bald cypress, although mature specimens in the wild may have an irregular shape. Its needles lie closely along the twigs and are not as feathery as those of bald cypress.

AT A GLANCE

Plant type: deciduous tree

Features: conical shape, needlelike leaves, golden fall color

Foliage: deciduous

Height: 50 to 70 feet

Light: full sun to partial shade

Soil: tolerates wide range

Water: medium

Problems: spider mites, bagworms

Native: Southeastern and South Central United States

Range: Zones 4 to 9

Remarks: grows quickly

Beard-tongue
Penstemon digitalis 'Husker Red'

Husker Red beard-tongue is one of the more than 250 species of native North American and Mexican beard-tongues known for their colorful flower spikes that bloom from late spring until fall. Named for the University of Nebraska Cornhuskers, Husker Red beard-tongue is a visual treat even when it is not in bloom, thanks to its unusual maroon-red foliage.

In the Landscape

This plant's striking foliage emerges in spring, followed in early to midsummer by translucent, white tubular flowers slightly tinted pink. Husker Red beard-tongue reaches a height of almost 3 feet.

Like other beard-tongues, this perennial brings a delicate, airy quality to a flower border or a naturalized setting. Its striking foliage also contrasts well with other garden perennials, such as coreopsis (page 138).

Planting and Care

Plant Husker Red beard-tongue in full sun or partial shade, and provide moist, well-drained soil. It requires little fertilizer. If cut back after flowering, this plant will bloom again, sometimes flowering into early winter in mild climates. To eliminate staking, pinch Husker Red beard-tongue to 8 inches when it is 12 inches high. This selection multiplies rapidly and should be divided periodically to

Husker Red beard-tongue has more going for it than pretty flowers. Colorful foliage also adds to its charm.

maintain vigor.

This species grows well in hot summers and thrives in the South.

Species and Selections

The most popular related species is common beard-tongue, *P. barbatus*, for which there are 30 to 40 named selections, that differ in flower color. This plant is the hardiest of the commonly available beardtongues, handling winters in Zone 3.

Selections include 'Alba' with white flowers, and 'Bashful', which has orange flowers. 'Crystal' sports white blooms, while 'Elfin Pink' has clear pink tubular-shaped flowers.

AT A GLANCE

Plant Type: perennial

Features: maroon-red foliage

Colors: white flowers

Height: 30 to 36 inches

Light: full sun

Soil: well drained

Water: medium

Problems: none specific

Native: North America

Range: Zones 3 to 8

Remarks: works well in informal gardens

Black Tupelo
Nyssa sylvatica

Every autumn without fail, you can count on the leaves of black tupelo to turn brilliant shades of orange, scarlet, and maroon. Also known as sour gum or black gum, black tupelo is native to the United States from Maine to Florida and west to Texas. An excellent ornamental tree, black tupelo is often found in the woodlands, and especially near or bordering lakes, streams, or swamps.

In the Landscape

Black tupelo is a large, deciduous shade tree that reaches a height of 30 to 50 feet and a spread of 25 to 30 feet. Young trees are cone shaped, but as they mature, the crown becomes more irregular and flatter, and they take on a more spreading character.

The foliage is a dark glossy green on the surface and a grayer green underneath. Although the flowers are harder to see because of the foliage, they are followed by blue-black berries in September or October that attract birds and animals.

The most outstanding feature of this native tree is its fall color. The leaves of black tupelo change from yellow to brilliant scarlet and then to a deep maroon in late fall. The tree's hallmark horizontal branching character is especially distinctive during winter.

Planting and Care

Black tupelo is propagated from seed and grown in

The leaves of Black Tupelo turn brilliant shades of red in the fall.

containers. For best results, choose a 6-foot nursery-grown tree, and plant it in full sun or partial shade.

Black tupelo prefers well-drained, moist, and slightly acidic soil. It can't tolerate alkaline soils. Although this tree suffers from many leaf problems, none are serious.

Species and Selections

Very few selections of tupelo exist, although form and fall color vary widely in the species.

Other native species of black tupelo are water tupelo (*N. aquatica*) and Ogeechee tupelo (*N. ogeche*). Water tupelo, like black tupelo, gives dependable fall color and is native to the swampy and wet regions from Eastern Virginia to Texas.

AT A GLANCE

Plant type: deciduous tree

Features: vivid red fall color, blue-black berries, horizontal branches

Height: 30 to 50 feet

Light: full sun to partial shade

Soil: well drained, moist, acidic

Water: medium

Problems: leaf problems

Native: United States

Range: Zones 3 to 9

Remarks: leaves appear shiny or wet

Black-eyed Susan
Rudbeckia fulgida var. *sullivantii* 'Goldsturm'

During the summer, the bright blooms of black-eyed Susan dot the landscape from Pennsylvania to Michigan and as far south as Texas and Florida. Gardeners everywhere love this daisy-like perennial because it is easy to grow and requires little care. The unmistakable yellow flowers with black "eyes" appear in July and provide a nonstop show of color until frost.

In the Landscape

Black-eyed Susan is a classic plant for a sunny flower border. Its vivid golden yellow petals and contrasting black centers provide superb visual impact in the garden.

Black-eyed Susan reaches a height of 2 to 3 feet at maturity, and it sports 2- to 3-inch wide blooms. Although this plant flowers in the summer, the blossoms will last into fall if the dead flowers are removed. Cut flowers are excellent in floral arrangements. Black-eyed Susan's brilliant color is especially effective when paired with butterfly weed (page 38), purple coneflower (page 108), or spike gayfeather (page 126).

Planting and Care

For maximum flowering, plant black-eyed Susan in full sun in moist, well-drained soil. This perennial multiplies quickly and at times may become invasive. To avoid this, divide the clumps in spring to

Mix black-eyed Susan with other bright-colored flowers, such as butterfly weed or purple coneflower.

keep it in bounds. This selection is best propagated by division and is rarely bothered by pests.

Species and Selections

Many related selections of black-eyed Susan are available in garden centers.

'Goldilocks', 'Gloriosa', 'Irish Eyes', 'Marmalade', and 'Sputnik' are a few named selections of *R. fulgida* var. *pulcherrima*. Although these flowers are in the same family as 'Goldsturm', they have patterning on their yellow blooms.

Other native species that are popular for flower gardens are cutleaf coneflower (*R. laciniata*) and black-eyed Susan (*R. hirta*). 'Indian

Summer', a new selection of *R. hirta*, is an annual that has been successfully grown at Callaway Gardens in Georgia.

AT A GLANCE

Plant type: perennial

Features: daisylike summer blooms

Colors: deep yellow flowers with black centers

Height: 2 to 3 feet

Light: full sun

Soil: moist, well drained, fertile

Water: medium during summer

Problems: none specific

Native: North America

Range: Zones 3 to 9

Remarks: carefree perennial with rapid growth

Blue Wild Indigo

Baptisia australis

Blue wild indigo produces dainty flowers on tall spikes from mid- to late-spring to early summer. The plant's Latin name comes from the Greek word *bapto*, which means "to dye." A member of the pea family, blue wild indigo is native to the Eastern United States from Pennsylvania south to Georgia.

In the Landscape

This native species grows in open, dry woods. Its gray-green foliage appears in early spring, followed by spikes of indigo flowers in mid- to late-spring, which last for almost a month.

Blue wild indigo can grow to a height of 3 feet, making this perennial an ideal candidate for the middle or back of a flower border. It is also good for areas with erosion problems.

After the first frost, its leaves turn coal black, revealing the seed pods, which last until late fall. After the seeds ripen, the pods rattle when shaken. They can be removed as they mature and planted. Scrape the seeds with sandpaper before planting to allow water and oxygen to penetrate the seed's outer layer.

Planting and Care

Blue wild indigo flourishes in a wide variety of soil conditions, but it won't tolerate lime. For maximum flowering, this plant needs full sun and deep soil. For an extended blooming season, faded flowers should be

The tall spikes of blue wild indigo tower over the border, reaching a height of 3 feet.

removed. Although the plant adapts to partial shade, staking is needed and the blooms are not as dramatic.

Since this plant spreads by underground rhizomes, allow plenty of room for growth. Blue wild indigo can be propagated by dividing it in late fall to early spring. When first planted, this perennial may be slow to flower, but once established, it blooms freely.

Species and Selections

White-flowered species that grow well include white wild indigo (*B. alba*), prairie wild indigo (*B. leucantha*), and wild white indigo (*B. pendula*). Plains wild indigo (*B. leucophaea*) also has creamy white flowers.

AT A GLANCE

Plant type: perennial

Features: spring blooms, gray-green foliage

Colors: blue flowers

Height: 3 feet

Light: full sun to partial shade

Soil: wide range

Water: medium during summer months

Problems: none specific

Native: Eastern United States

Range: Zones 3 to 9

Remarks: not invasive, but allow plenty of growing room

Bluestar

Amsonia tabernaemontana

If you're looking for a resilient plant that will adapt to just about any growing conditions, don't overlook bluestar. Also known as willow amsonia, bluestar is perhaps the most carefree of native American wildflowers. Its star-shaped blue flowers unfold in late spring to early summer, lasting for two to four weeks. The show continues in the fall when it boasts bright golden foliage.

In the Landscape

Few perennials possess bluestar's versatility. This plant blooms well in either sun or light shade and will flourish year after year without being divided. It works well in borders, or in a woodland garden, and its blue flowers are effective when paired with peonies, irises, columbines, lamb's-ears, and tulips.

Planting and Care

This perennial grows best in full sun to partial shade in deep, moist soil with a moderate amount of fertilizer. During periods of drought, it requires more water. To keep plants compact, cut them back after flowering. Shade plants may need to be pruned to about half their height once a year to prevent them from growing too leggy. You can also grow shade plants through a circular support to keep them from toppling.

Although often underutilized, bluestar is a versatile perennial that needs little care.

Species and Selections

Downy amsonia (*A. angustifolia* syn. *ciliata*) is a related North American species with pale blue flowers and golden yellow fall foliage. Another native species, Arkansas amsonia (*A. ubrectii*), is a superior garden perennial. This species is sometimes hard to find at local nurseries, but it is often available from specialty catalogs. Louisiana bluestar (*A. ludoviciana*) is native to Southern Louisiana only and is distinguished by the white wool-like coating on the undersides of the leaves.

AT A GLANCE

Plant type: perennial

Features: delicate blue blooms in spring

Colors: blue flowers, golden foliage

Height: 2 to 3 feet

Light: full sun to partial shade

Soil: moderately fertile, moist

Water: medium during summer

Problems: none specific

Native: Southern and Midwestern United States

Range: Zones 3 to 9

Remarks: carefree woodland plant

Blue-Mist Shrub

Caryopteris x clandonensis

Blue-mist shrub creates a drift of bright blue flowers in the landscape in late summer. Also called blue-beard or blue spirea, this ornamental shrub offers a splash of garden color when few other deciduous plants are in bloom.

In the Landscape

This shrub is a low-growing, graceful plant that grows 2 feet high in one season. It works well in the front of a perennial border and complements the bright yellow and orange colors of calendulas, marigolds and zinnias. Its gray-green foliage contrasts well with the blue flowers.

Because of its low growth habit, blue-mist shrub can also be enjoyed as an indoor potted plant if given adequate light.

Planting and Care

Blue-mist shrub is a carefree plant. To attain maximum flowering, plant it in full sun in loose, loamy, organic soil with adequate moisture. Since this shrub blooms on new growth, it should be cut back to the ground in late fall or early winter. If left unpruned, blue-mist shrub may be killed back by severe winters. If it survives the winter, severe pruning in spring usually encourages it to flower again. Once pruned, provide a handful of granular fertilizer at the base of the shrub.

Plant blue-mist shrub in the front of a border for a dash of late-summer color.

Species and Selections

In the 1930s, gardener Arthur Simmonds produced the original hybrid of the species, called 'Arthur Simmonds'. Selections include 'Heavenly Blue', a plant with a more compact form and deeper blue flowers than the species. 'Longwood Blue', a selection created at Longwood Gardens in Pennsylvania, is taller and has lavender-blue flowers.

The species *incana*, or common bluebeard, is not as cold tolerant as blue-mist shrub, but it is popular for its small, violet-blue flowers.

AT A GLANCE

Plant type: deciduous shrub

Features: gray-green foliage, late-summer blooms

Colors: bright blue flowers

Height: 2 feet

Light: full sun for best flowering

Soil: loamy, organic

Water: medium

Problems: none specific

Native: hybrid

Range: Zones 6 to 9

Remarks: prune to ground in late fall or early winter

Bottlebrush Buckeye

Aesculus parviflora

No matter which season, bottlebrush buckeye puts on a colorful show. Long, white flowers appear in late June and July, followed by bright yellow foliage in the fall. Its distinctive leaves, which are green the rest of the year, resemble a hand with its fingers spread.

In the Landscape

Bottlebrush buckeye is a versatile shrub that works well as a single plant or in mass plantings. It reaches a height and width of 8 to 12 feet.

This species produces orange buckeye seeds that fade to brown as the fruit matures. These seeds can be used for propagation, but they should not be allowed to dry out before they are planted.

Commonly found in the Southeastern United States from South Carolina to Alabama and Florida, bottlebrush buckeye is a good choice for a woodland garden.

Planting and Care

For maximum flowering, plant this shrub in full sun, providing adequate water. Although it will bloom in partial shade, the flowers will not be as profuse. Well-drained, slightly acidic, organic soil is ideal for growth. This shrub is pest-free and requires little maintenance.

Bottlebrush buckeye spreads by suckers, shoots that grow from the roots or beneath the surface of the ground. The suckers can easily be pruned back if desired.

Wands of feathery white flowers (right) give bottlebrush buckeye its name. Its foliage turns a sunny yellow in the fall (above).

Species and Selections

'Rogers', a named selection cultivated in Urbana, Illinois, has flowers more than twice as long as those of the species.

Another plant related to bottlebrush buckeye is red buckeye (*A. pavia*), a treelike shrub with 8-inch spikes of bright red spring flowers. Painted buckeye (*A. sylvatica*) has multicolored flowers. Common horse chestnut, (*A. hippocastanum*), is a shrub that prefers the colder climates of Zones 3 to 7 and grows as tall as 75 feet. After the foliage has emerged, upright flower spikes 10 inches long cover the tips of the branches.

AT A GLANCE

Plant type: shrub

Features: feathery summer blooms, bright autumn foliage

Colors: white flowers

Height: 8 to 12 feet

Light: full sun to partial shade

Soil: slightly acidic, organic

Water: medium; will die in drought

Problems: none specific

Native: Southeastern United States

Range: Zones 4 to 9

Remarks: produces "buckeye" fruits similar to the shrub horse chestnut

Bougainvillea Goldenrain Tree

Koelreuteria bipinnata

Bougainvillea goldenrain tree, with its cloud of yellow flowers, is one of the most beautiful ornamental trees. It brings a burst of color to the landscape when other summer-flowering trees and shrubs are waning. Shortly after flowering, the tree bears striking reddish bronze seed pods, whose color lasts for several weeks. Their beauty can be enjoyed in dried floral arrangements, too, because cut pods retain their hue for years.

In the Landscape

A native of China, bougainvillea goldenrain tree reaches a height of 20 to 30 feet in 10 to 15 years. Although a mature tree is wider than it is tall, it takes more than 15 years to reach its maximum spread. The tree's upright, umbrella shape makes it an excellent candidate for terraces, patios, or anywhere you want to create light shade.

Planting and Care

For best flowering, plant bougainvillea goldenrain tree in full sun. Although this tree will grow in almost any type of soil, good drainage is essential. Once the roots are established, it tolerates drought and thrives without much care.

As a young tree, bougainvillea goldenrain tree often has an ungainly appearance. Pruning the branches at this stage encourages good branch structure, although it takes

While in bloom, bougainvillea goldenrain tree sports bright yellow flowers (right). Bronze-toned seed pods appear after the flowers fade (above).

five to six years for the tree's lateral spread to lose its awkwardness.

Species and Selections

'Flamegold' (*K. elegans*) is a similar ornamental species that has little cold tolerance and should only be grown in Zones 9 to 11. On the Pacific island of Fiji, the leaves of this tree were boiled to produce black hair dye.

The most widely grown species is goldenrain tree (*K. paniculata*). One of the earliest cultivated trees in China, it was often planted on tombs of scholars. This species bears clusters of small yellow flowers in early summer and fares well in Zones 5 to 9. The greenish seed pods, which appear after the flowers, add to the summer display.

AT A GLANCE

Plant type: deciduous tree

Features: late-summer blooms with colorful seed pods, umbrella shape

Colors: deep yellow flowers

Height: 20 to 30 feet

Light: full sun

Soil: tolerates wide range

Water: medium

Problems: none serious

Native: China

Range: Zones 7 to 10

Remarks: drought tolerant

Bumald Spirea

Spiraea x bumalda

A staple in older gardens, bumald spirea is an old-fashioned plant that requires little care. Along with forsythia, weigela, and winter honeysuckle, bumald spirea is a graceful dwarf shrub with profuse summer flowers.

In the Landscape

While most spireas are large, arching shrubs, bumald spirea has a compact growth habit. It will reach 2 to 3 feet in height, with a spread of 3 to 5 feet in two to three years.

Bumald spirea is often used in mass plantings, although many of the newer selections make a colorful accent in a flower border. The shrub flowers in summer, with blossoms that range in color from white to pink. Bumald spirea's leaves are pinkish red when they unfold, and they later change to dark blue-green. Other selections have chartreuse to yellow foliage.

Planting and Care

Like other spireas, bumald spirea is a hardy, tough plant. Although it can tolerate a fair amount of shade, it needs full sun for more profuse blooms. Bumald spirea endures a wide range of soil conditions, including heavy clay, provided it has good drainage.

For larger flower clusters, prune the plant in early spring before the leaves appear. If deadheads are removed after flowering, this shrub may bloom again in late summer.

Bumald spirea has blue-green leaves in spring (above) and produces deep pink flowers in summer (right).

Species and Selections

The most popular selection of low-growing, reddish pink flowering spireas is 'Anthony Waterer'. Its leaves vary in color from a mottled yellow to solid yellow and it tolerates heat and drought well.

Bridal wreath spirea (*S. prunifolia*), a related species, has small, white, button-sized flowers that distinguish it from other spireas. It is also one of the few spireas with orange to red autumn foliage.

Developed before 1868, Vanhouttei spirea (*S. x vanhouttei*) is a fast-growing species that works well as an informal flowering hedge. It can grow as tall as 8 feet, with a spread of 10 feet, so give it plenty of room to grow. This spirea has a vase-shaped growth habit with arching branches that curve to the ground.

AT A GLANCE

Plant type: deciduous shrub

Features: continuous summer blooms

Colors: white to pink flowers

Height: 2 to 3 feet

Light: full sun

Soil: tolerates wide range with good drainage

Water: medium

Problems: none specific

Native: hybrid origin

Range: Zones 3 to 8

Remarks: many selections have distinctly colored foliage

Burkwood viburnum
Viburnum x *burkwoodii*

Choosing just one viburnum from the 70 species available can be difficult. They vary widely in form, flowers, and appearance. Burkwood viburnum, a hybrid of two species, is best known for its spicy, fragrant flowers that bloom from early spring to late summer. Almost evergreen in warmer climates, burkwood viburnum is deciduous in cooler zones.

In the Landscape

Burkwood viburnum has a loose, irregular, vase-shaped form, and can reach a height of 8 to 10 feet. The showy, early-spring blooms have pink buds that open to reveal white flowers.

To fully appreciate this shrub, plant it against a dense evergreen background to minimize the sparseness of its leaves in fall. Choose a location where the heady scent from the blooms can be enjoyed.

Planting and Care

For best flowering, plant burkwood viburnum in full sun to partial shade. In dense shade, it becomes leggy and flowers poorly. This shrub prefers moist, well-drained soil that is fertile, yet slightly acidic.

Like other viburnums, this variety is susceptible to leaf spot and occasional insect problems. To minimize damage, spray the plant with an insecticide. An occasional pruning will help improve the shrub's looks.

When it comes to large, fragrant white blooms, burkwood viburnum is an excellent choice for the garden.

Species and Selections

In the past few years, growers have produced new selections of burkwood viburnum. 'Chenaultii', a selection introduced by the National Arboretum, produces impressive flower displays, while 'Mohawk' features fragrant flowers that turn from red to white.

Other ornamental species include Linden viburnum (*V. dilatatum*), which bears red fruit and red to purple leaves in fall, and doublefile viburnum (*V. plicatum* var. *tomentosum*), a small 15- to 20-foot tree with vivid scarlet color and red berries in fall.

The largest snowball variety is Chinese snowball (*V. macrocephalum*), a plant with blooms that measure 5-inches wide.

AT A GLANCE

Plant type: semievergreen shrub

Features: fragrant spring blooms

Colors: white flowers

Height: 8 to 10 feet

Light: full sun to partial shade

Soil: moist, well drained, fertile, slightly acidic

Water: medium

Problems: leaf spot

Native: hybrid origin

Range: Zones 4 to 8

Remarks: almost evergreen in warmer climates

Butterfly Bush
Buddleia davidii

Butterfly bush is an old-fashioned shrub prized for flowers that draw butterflies and hummingbirds to the garden. A mainstay of any butterfly garden, this deciduous shrub brings a colorful display of lavender hues to the summer garden, but with an extra measure of appeal—butterflies.

In the Landscape

Butterfly bush is known for its speedy growth. Depending on the selection, it can reach 10 to 15 feet high and 10 feet wide in as little as five to seven years, so be sure to give it plenty of growing room.

Often used in mass as part of a shrub or perennial border, butterfly bush reaches its peak in the summer when the fragrant flowers burst into bloom. The blossoms attract a wide array of native butterflies to drink their nectar. There are many different flower colors, depending on the selection, but most are various shades of purple, pink, white, blue, or yellow.

Planting and Care

Butterfly bush grows vigorously in most garden soil. To encourage better flowering, plant this shrub in full sun in well-drained, fertile soil. Blooms appear in early summer, and if deadheads are removed, flowering will extend until frost.

In colder climates, butterfly bush is often treated as a herbaceous perennial rather than

A butterfly sips the nectar from the delicate flowers of butterfly bush (right). The purple flower spikes dramatically shoot up from the shrub (above).

as a deciduous woody shrub. Because this plant blooms on new growth, it should be cut back to the ground at the end of the growing season. This encourages new, vigorous growth in spring.

Species and Selections

There are more than 70 hybrids of butterfly bush available.

'African Queen', one of the more popular selections, has dark violet flowers. Other favorites include 'DuBonnet', which has dark purple flowers, and 'White Bouquet', which sports white flowers and orange centers. 'Royal Red', which was introduced in China in 1900, has purple-red

flowers with orange centers and is now widely grown in the United States.

AT A GLANCE

Plant type: deciduous shrub

Features: fragrant early-summer blooms on long spikes

Colors: lilac flowers with orange centers

Height: 10 to 15 feet

Light: full sun

Soil: well drained, fertile

Water: medium

Problems: none specific

Native: China

Range: Zones 5 to 9

Remarks: vigorous and hardy

Butterfly Weed

Asclepias tuberosa

Every summer, the bright orange flowers of butterfly weed grow in the most unlikely places, especially along railroad tracks. This wildflower perennial is a host plant for butterflies, particularly the monarch. This insect feeds almost exclusively on members of the milkweed family, to which butterfly weed belongs.

More than 150 years ago, the soft, downy seeds of butterfly weed were used instead of feathers as stuffing in beds and cushions.

In the Landscape

Although butterfly weed will grow anywhere, this plant loves the deep, rich soil of a flower bed. Its brightly colored orange flowers blend well with other vibrant colors, such as bright yellow, blue, burgundy, magenta, or red.

Butterfly weed is valued as a cut flower because of its longevity. For best results, cut the blooms early in the morning or at night, and place the stems in water high enough to reach the flowers.

This species is native from New Hampshire to Minnesota, south to Florida, and as far west as Arizona and New Mexico.

Planting and Care

Although it may be tempting to dig these plants from the wild, resist the temptation to do so. Butterfly weed develops large taproots, making it difficult to transplant. Instead, collect a few seeds from the

Combine the bold orange flowers of butterfly weed with other vibrant colors (above). You will often find butterfly weed growing wild (right).

mature pods in late summer. You can also buy the seed from catalogs, or purchase plants from nurseries that grow native American wildflowers. Butterfly weed can also be propagated from root cuttings. Once established, it will produce large, flowering clumps if given full sun and well-drained soil.

Species and Selections

There are several species of native American milkweeds that are ornamental and serve as host plants for butterflies. Swamp milkweed, *A. incarnata*, has pink to mauve to white flowers and grows 3 feet tall. Common milkweed, *A. syriaca*, has green to purplish flowers that are followed by seed pods.

AT A GLANCE

Plant type: perennial

Features: brilliant summer flowers

Colors: red, yellow, and orange

Height: 18 to 36 inches

Light: full sun

Soil: well-drained, moderately fertile

Water: low to medium

Problems: none specific

Native: Eastern United States

Range: Zones 4 to 9

Remarks: attracts large numbers of butterflies

Canadian Hemlock

Tsuga canadensis

Canadian hemlock is a versatile landscape plant, filling the role of specimen tree, a clipped hedge, or a private screen. Its fine-textured foliage and graceful form is found in the Eastern United States and Canada from Nova Scotia to Minnesota, and south to the northern portions of Alabama and Georgia.

In the Landscape

Canadian hemlock grows in a conical shape, reaching a height of 40 to 70 feet; its branches spread in an elegant fashion, reaching from 25 to 30 feet.

Use Canadian hemlock as a tall understory tree, a windbreak, or an evergreen screen. It can even be sheared into a formal hedge, although this will require regular trimming. Because of its size, be sure to plant the tree at least 20 feet away from the house and a safe distance from power lines.

Planting and Care

Canadian hemlock grows well in deep shade, although its form will not be as dense. For best results, plant this tree in partial shade. In the North, Canadian hemlock grows well in full sun, but in areas where summer temperatures exceed 95 degrees, the foliage suffers from sunscald and dieback.

Plant Canadian hemlock in moist, well-drained, organic soil that is slightly acidic. This tree is susceptible to drought and requires extra water dur-

The small cones that dangle from the needled branches of Canadian hemlock hold the tree's seeds (above). Plant several trees together and prune them into a formal shrub (right).

ing the summer months. In the North, Canadian hemlock is attacked by the insect wooly adelgid, which causes the needles to drop.

Species and Selections

There are more than 40 named selections of Canadian hemlock that differ in form and growth habit. 'Bennett' has weeping branches, and 'Sargentii' has a broad-spreading, weeping form.

A related species, Carolina hemlock, *T. caroliniana*, is native to the Southeastern United States. It tolerates harsh city conditions, such as compacted soil and foot traffic, better than Canadian hemlock.

AT A GLANCE

Plant type: evergreen tree

Features: fine-textured needles, graceful form

Colors: dark green needles, brown cones

Height: 40 to 70 feet

Light: full sun to deep shade

Soil: moist, well drained, organic, slightly acidic

Water: medium, intolerant of drought

Problems: wooly adelgid in northern range

Native: North America

Range: Zones 3 to 7

Remarks: good for screening

Cardinal Flower
Lobelia cardinalis

Cardinal flower brings brilliant red color and height to the garden.

The history of cardinal flower can be traced back almost four centuries. Cultivated in Europe since the early 1600s, it was one of the first wildflowers sent to the United States.

Named for the scarlet robes worn by cardinals in the Roman Catholic church, the bright red flower spikes of this perennial are a favorite of hummingbirds and bees. It grows from Southeastern Canada to the Gulf Coast states of the South.

In the Landscape

Cardinal flower is at home in a variety of locations. It works well in a flower border, along a stream, or part of a naturalized woodland garden.

This plant performs best, however, beside a partially shaded stream or pool, a setting similar to its native habitat. It is often seen near the edges of cypress swamps, in rich bottomlands, and on the banks of streams in Southern states. The red flowers blend well with native ferns and the flower spikes make excellent cut flowers.

Planting and Care

Cardinal flower needs rich, organic, moist soil for best growth. In the deep South, plant this perennial in partial shade. If your garden lacks shade, be sure to provide the plant with plenty of moisture.

Cardinal flower is self-sowing if the seedheads are allowed to mature on the plant. Seedlings are easy to transplant to new locations. Although this perennial is short-lived, seedlings or offshoots prolong the plant's presence in the garden.

Species and Selections

A few named selections are available, including 'Alba', which has white flowers, and 'Heather Pink', which bears soft pink flowers. Big blue lobelia (*L. syphilitica*), a related species, features soft pale blue flowers that appear later in the fall. Selections include 'Blue Peter'.

Growers have created many hybrids with unusual red leaves by crossing *L. cardinalis* with *L. syphilitica* and *L. splendens*. 'Queen Victoria' has red flowers and bronze foliage and reaches a height of 5 feet, while 'Bee's Flame' has vermillion red flowers and deep red foliage.

AT A GLANCE

Plant Type: perennial

Features: tall flower spikes appear in midsummer and fall

Colors: red

Height: 2 to 4 feet

Light: partial shade

Soil: rich, organic

Water: medium to high

Problems: none specific

Native: Eastern North America

Range: Zones 2 to 9

Remarks: attracts hummingbirds; long blooming time

Chinese Elm

Ulmus parviflora

If you have visited Walt Disney World in Orlando, Florida, you have seen Chinese elm trees lining the streets. This disease-resistant shade tree is known for its attractive peeling bark, which gives it its other common name, lacebark elm. As the tree matures, the bark peels away to reveal unusual patterns underneath. This tree is often confused with Siberian elm (*U. pumila*), an inferior species with brittle bark.

In the Landscape

Chinese elm is deciduous, but in the warmer areas of Zones 9 and 10, the tree can be evergreen. Many selections have a graceful, weeping form, while others are more upright and vase-shaped, like American elm.

Chinese elm grows quickly, easily reaching a height of 40 to 50 feet in 15 to 20 years. Young trees can grow as much as 3 feet per year if given good growing conditions.

This tree is an excellent choice for a street planting or for lining a driveway or long walkway. Chinese elm also works well in narrow courtyards, where shade is needed. It's also a natural for decks, terraces, and porches.

Planting and Care

Because it endures hot, dry conditions, Chinese elm is an excellent choice for cities. Its compact root system enables it to grow well in narrow areas such as parking lot islands,

Chinese elm's graceful branches create a pool of shade (right). The scaly bark peels off to reveal unusual patterns underneath (above).

medians, sidewalks, and other spaces that need shade.

For best growth, plant this tree in full sun, although it can tolerate shady locations. It prefers moist, fertile soil and tolerates both alkaline and acidic soil. Balled-and-burlapped trees transplant well.

Species and Selections

Selections popular for their superior form include 'Dynasty', 'Emerald Isle', 'Emerald Vase', and 'Prairie Shade', a selection from Oklahoma.

'Drake', 'Sempervirens', and 'True Green' are more cold-sensitive selections that should be grown only in Zones 7 to 9. 'Drake' has sweeping, pendulous branches and deep green foliage. 'Sempervirens' has a rounded crown and a spreading form, while 'True Green' tends to be almost evergreen and more rounded in habit.

AT A GLANCE

Plant type: deciduous tree

Features: shade tree with beautiful mottled bark

Foliage: deciduous

Height: 40 to 50 feet

Light: full sun to partial shade

Soil: moist, well drained

Water: medium

Problems: none specific

Native: China, Japan, Korea

Range: Zones 4 to 9

Remarks: excellent disease resistance, tolerates urban conditions

Chinese Fringe Tree
Chionanthus retusus

Native to the Orient, Chinese fringe tree drips with white blooms in late spring. Although not as common as white fringe tree, Chinese fringe tree is a beautiful version of the species that can be found in specialty nurseries.

In the Landscape

Chinese fringe tree has a multitrunked form similar to that of crepe myrtle (page 52). It grows in a rounded, irregular manner and can reach a height of 15 to 25 feet in 20 to 25 years.

One of this tree's most notable assets is its drooping, fringelike white flowers, which cover the tree from late April to May and last for several weeks.

A member of the olive family, the female plants of this tree produce blue-black fruit that mature in late September and October. In late fall, the foliage turns golden yellow.

Chinese fringe tree is at home in naturalistic settings and makes a good specimen tree. It is also an ideal choice for urban settings because it tolerates air pollution.

Planting and Care

For best flowering and growth, plant Chinese fringe tree in full sun in moist, fertile, organic soil that is slightly acidic. Balled-and-burlapped specimens should be planted in early spring before new foliage emerges.

In late spring, Chinese fringe tree is covered in white blossoms that last for several weeks.

Species and Selections

White fringe tree (*C. virginicus*), a related species, is native to the Eastern United States from New Jersey to Florida and west to Texas. It is often called old man's beard or grancy graybeard.

This species also produces cascades of white late-spring flowers, however, the blooms are longer in length than those of Chinese fringe tree. It is one of the last trees to produce leaves in the spring. New plants do not bloom until they are three to five years old.

A dwarf form of Chinese fringe tree, *C. pygmaeus*, is often grown in Florida.

AT A GLANCE

Plant type: deciduous tree

Features: clusters of white spring blooms, yellow fall color, multitrunked form

Height: 15 to 25 feet

Light: full sun

Soil: moist, fertile, slightly acidic

Water: medium

Problems: none specific

Native: China, Japan, Korea

Range: Zones 5 to 8

Remarks: male and female plants are separate

Chinese Pistachio

Pistacia chinensis

There are many reasons to plant Chinese pistachio. A native of China, this hardy tree is an ideal city tree because it thrives under difficult growing conditions, including compacted soil and drought. It is undemanding and requires little care. In autumn, this deciduous tree colors the landscape with its brilliant hues of red, orange, and gold.

In the Landscape

Chinese pistachio can reach a height of 30 to 35 feet with a spread of 25 to 35 feet in 10 to 15 years. A young tree experiences an awkward stage, growing irregularly until fully mature. At maturity, it develops an attractive oval-shaped appearance, making it a good accent or specimen tree.

Like the holly (page 152), Chinese pistachio is a dioecious plant, meaning the male and female plants are separate. Male and female trees must be planted near each other for pollination to occur for fruit production. The female trees bear clusters of red and light blue fruit, which ripen in October. The blue fruit are viable for propagation. During the growing season, the foliage is dark green and turns a vibrant orange to orange-red in the fall.

Planting and Care

Chinese pistachio prefers full sun for best growth. Although the tree will tolerate partial shade, its fall color will not be as pronounced. This tree

Chinese pistachio leaves turn hues of orange and gold in the fall (right). Female trees bear clusters of light blue and red fruit (above).

endures a wide range of soil types, including clay, loamy, and sandy soil. If the soil is well drained, Chinese pistachio also tolerates alkaline and acidic pH conditions.

Species and Selections

'Keith Davey', a male selection, is easy to train and has exceptional fall color. The color differs among selections, so keep this in mind when purchasing. Seedlings of Chinese pistachio are often used for grafting the commercial pistachio tree, *P. vera*. This species is smaller, with slightly different leaves. It is native to Western Asia and is often grown in Mediterranean countries.

AT A GLANCE

Plant type: deciduous tree

Features: superior fall color, female plants produce fall fruit

Colors: red and light blue fruit

Height: 30 to 35 feet

Light: full sun to partial shade

Soil: well drained

Water: medium

Problems: none specific

Native: China

Range: Zones 6 to 9

Remarks: male and female plants; ideal for urban areas

Chinese Witch Hazel

Hamamelis mollis

When the promise of spring is still a few weeks away, Chinese witch hazel begins to uncurl its spidery yellow flowers. The popularity of this deciduous shrub has increased dramatically due to its unusual late-winter blooms.

In the Landscape

Chinese witch hazel is an almost treelike shrub, reaching a height of 10 to 15 feet in as many years. It has an oval to vase-shaped form with wide-spreading branches.

For year-round enjoyment, highlight Chinese witch hazel by providing it with an evergreen background. It looks best when planted at the edge of a wooded area or in a natural setting. In fall, the leaves turn yellow to orange, providing contrast.

Planting and Care

Chinese witch hazel is a carefree plant with no serious pest or disease problems. For best flowering, plant this shrub in full sun or partial shade and give it well-drained, organic, slightly acidic soil.

Many species of Chinese witch hazel keep their old foliage until new blooms appear. To improve the tree's appearance, remove the old, dried foliage when the shrub begins to flower in early spring.

This shrub is not as cold hardy as some other varieties. Occasionally, extreme cold temperatures in Zone 5 can kill the flower buds.

Chinese witch hazel reaches out with spidery fingers in a blaze of late-winter color.

Species and Selections

Common witch hazel, *H. virginiana*, a species native to the Eastern United States, bears fragrant pale yellow flowers in early October. Long ago, divining rods made from witch hazel branches were used to find underground water.

The named selections of this species offer a variety of yellow blooms. 'Brevipetala' has deep yellow flowers, 'Early Bright' has bright yellow, early-blooming flowers, and 'Pallida' produces soft yellow flowers. The hybrid *H. x intermedia* is just as popular. Selections include 'Arnold's Promise' and 'Sunburst', which sport yellow flowers, and 'Diane' and 'Ruby Glow', which have bright coppery-red flowers. 'Jelena' produces copper flowers with orange centers.

AT A GLANCE

Plant type: deciduous shrub

Features: fragrant, late-winter blooms; yellow to orange fall color

Colors: yellow to copper flowers

Height: 10 to 15 feet

Light: full sun to partial shade

Soil: well drained, organic

Water: medium

Problems: none specific

Native: China

Range: Zones 5 to 8

Remarks: remove old foliage when shrub begins to flower

Crepe Myrtle
Lagerstroemia indica

The colorful flowers of crepe myrtle seem oblivious to the summer heat as they stretch open their blossoms to the sun. Native to China and Korea, crepe myrtle gets its name from the soft crepe paperlike flowers that appear in abundance throughout the summer.

In the Landscape

Crepe myrtle is a versatile landscape plant that is available in many heights and flower colors and adapts to many growing conditions. Its size varies from dwarf to medium, and most trees have three or more trunks.

Mature specimens easily reach a height of 15 to 25 feet in 10 to 12 years, but older ones can grow well over 40 feet. The flowers of crepe myrtle are white, varying shades of pink, watermelon red, or lavender.

Crepe myrtle is also prized for its smooth, sculptured bark, which peels off to reveal elegant shades of brown underneath. In the fall, the foliage turns brilliant shades of yellow, orange, or red. Choose small selections of crepe myrtle where space is restricted, and reserve the larger trees to shade a patio or to create a screen.

Planting and Care

Crepe myrtle thrives in a wide variety of horticultural conditions, provided it has good drainage. For maximum flowering, plant this tree in full

Crepe myrtle grows easily in the narrow strip between a curb and a sidewalk (above). The soft flowers cover the tree throughout the summer (right).

sun. Crepe myrtle is often severely pruned to promote large flower heads; however, light pruning is best to help the tree retain its form and to increase blooming. Remove stems no thicker than a pencil to encourage branching and flowering.

Species and Selections

Selections include 'Near East' and 'Biloxi', which have pale pink flowers, 'Carolina Beauty' and 'William Toovey', which have red flowers, and 'Glendora White' and 'White Cloud', which sport white flowers. To avoid leaf problems, choose mildew-resistant hybrids, such as 'Muskogee', 'Tuscarora', and 'Natchez'.

AT A GLANCE

Plant type: deciduous tree

Features: abundant white to pink summer blooms, sculptured bark

Height: 15 to 25 feet

Light: full sun

Soil: wide range of soil conditions

Water: medium

Problems: powdery mildew, aphids, leaf spot

Native: China, Korea

Range: Zones 7 to 9

Remarks: long-lived, showy flowers; good for small spaces; needs good drainage

Crocosmia

Crocosmia x 'Lucifer'

Crocosmia 'Lucifer' gets its name from the color red's association with the devil. Its bright blooms are suspended on the ends of spiky stems, appearing like pitchforks and withstanding even the highest temperatures in Zone 9. But that's where the similarity with the devil ends. This summer-blooming bulb is a member of the iris family, with foliage similar to gladioli.

Created by Bloom Nurseries in Bressingham, England, this bulb often appears in catalogs under the name montbretia.

The blazing blooms of crocosmia, with their long, spiky stems, are prized for cutting (right). The tubular-shaped flowers are a favorite of hummingbirds (above).

In the Landscape

Crocosmia's graceful, arching form makes this plant well-suited for the back of the flower border. Its bold orange to orange-red tubular flowers, which appear in late June or July, mix well with other bright flowers, such as purple coneflower (page 108). For an eye-catching display of color, plant these bulbs in mass.

Planting and Care

For best growth, this perennial requires rich, well-drained soil and plenty of sun. To keep plants from becoming crowded, divide them every two to three years.

Crocosmia also makes an ideal container plant. For best results, as the foliage emerges from the soil, fertilize every other week with a water-soluble fertilizer until flowering occurs.

Species and Selections

In addition to 'Lucifer', there are other named selections bred in England, including 'Emberglow', 'Spitfire', and 'Bressingham Blaze'.

South African species are golden coppertip, *C. aurea*, and hybrids of *C. aurea* and Pott's coppertip, *C. pottsii*, known as Tritonia pottsii or montbretia. Named selections of this hybrid include 'Citronella', 'His Majesty', 'Vesuvius', 'Emily McKenzie', 'Meteor', and 'Fire King'. These plants have larger blooms than Pott's coppertip, and range in color from orange to scarlet.

AT A GLANCE

Plant type: perennial (bulb)

Features: funnel-shaped flowers, swordlike foliage

Colors: bright orange, red

Height: foliage to 3 feet, flower sprays to 4 feet

Light: full sun

Soil: well drained, organic

Water: medium

Problems: none specific

Native: England

Range: Zones 5 to 9

Remarks: attracts hummingbirds

Dawn Redwood

Metasequoia glyptostroboides

While dinosaurs were on the verge of becoming extinct 50 million years ago, dawn redwood thrived in their world. But like the dinosaur, this tree was believed to have been extinct for a million years.

In 1941, this species was described from fossils found in Japan. In 1944, scientists discovered this tree growing wild in China. The same year, an expedition sponsored by the Arnold Arboretum in Boston brought seeds to the United States for distribution. Today, this tree is a living monument to a prehistoric time.

In the Landscape

Dawn redwood is a large, fast-growing deciduous tree that resembles the California redwood and bald cypress (page 14). It has an upright, pyramidal form and reaches a height of 50 feet in only 15 to 20 years. As the tree ages, the trunk becomes buttressed in appearance.

In the fall, the foliage turns an attractive orange-brown to reddish brown color. The fallen needles create a carpet of natural mulch underneath the tree.

This graceful ornamental tree is often used in Oriental-style landscapes, particularly near streams and ponds. It is also used for screening, in parks, on playgrounds, and in other large spaces.

The soft, needlelike leaves of dawn redwood resemble those of hemlock (above). Because it grows fast, it is not a tree for small spaces (right).

Planting and Care

To obtain a compact growth habit, plant dawn redwood in full sun. Although this tree will tolerate partial shade, it will will take on a loose form. It prefers moist, well-drained, slightly acidic soil with a high organic matter content.

Although dawn redwood is a low-maintenance tree, Japanese beetles will sometimes attack the foliage. To control these pests, thoroughly spray the leaves with an insecticide.

Species and Selections

This species includes two named selections that differ from dawn redwood in growth habit. 'National', bred by the National Arboretum, and 'Sheridan Spire' develop a narrower pyramidal form with maturity.

AT A GLANCE

Plant Type: deciduous tree

Features: small, needlelike leaves; superior fall color; brown shedding bark

Height: 40 to 50 feet

Light: full sun to partial shade

Soil: moist, well drained, slightly acidic

Water: medium

Problems: Japanese beetles

Native: China

Range: Zones 4 to 8

Remarks: rapid growth rate

Downy Serviceberry

Amelanchier arborea

Downy serviceberry is one of the first trees to bloom during spring. Its showy white flowers unfold in mid-March, signaling the approaching flower display of dogwoods and azaleas.

Legend has it that, in northern climates, winter funeral services were not held until the soil thawed enough to dig. The spring thaw coincided with the blooming of this tree, giving downy serviceberry its common name.

A native of the Eastern United States, downy serviceberry also goes by the name shadbush, because it usually blooms when shad fish swim to their spawning grounds in the rivers of New England.

In the Landscape

Downy serviceberry is often grown as a multistemmed large shrub or small tree. Most trees reach a height of 15 to 25 feet in 10 to 15 years. The lower leaves have a feathery, gray-green appearance.

In the deep South, white flowers appear in mid- to late-March. The flower show is short-lived, lasting only a week to 10 days. The blooms are followed by reddish purple berries that ripen in June and are consumed by birds. In fall, the tree's foliage takes on a color that ranges from yellow to orange.

Planting and Care

Downy serviceberry naturally occurs in wetlands to upland woods, so it grows best in

In full bloom before dogwoods and azaleas, downy serviceberry (right) foretells the coming of spring. In fall, it boasts vivid orange foliage (above).

moist, organic, slightly acidic soil. Although it tolerates full sun, partial shade is better, since in its native habitat it grows in the shadow of taller trees.

Downy serviceberry is susceptible to fire blight and leaf spot. To minimize damage, prune the affected foliage.

Species and Selections

Many selections are chosen for their flowering ability. Most are hybrids of downy serviceberry and another native, Allegheny serviceberry (*A. laevis*), listed as *A.* x *grandiflora*. This group includes 'Autumn Brilliance', 'Ballerina', and 'Princess Diana'.

AT A GLANCE

Plant type: deciduous tree

Features: late-winter to early-spring blooms, colorful fall foliage

Colors: white flowers, reddish purple berries

Height: 15 to 25 feet

Light: partial shade

Soil: moist, organic, slightly acidic

Water: medium

Problems: fire blight, leaf spot

Native: Eastern United States

Range: Zones 4 to 9

Remarks: birds feed on edible berries

Flowering Dogwood
Cornus florida

If there were a contest for a national tree, flowering dogwood would be a finalist. A colorful tree in all seasons, flowering dogwood grows in many areas in the Eastern United States, south from Massachusetts to Florida and west to Texas. Although this species grows in Zones 5 to 9, it's wise to choose a selection partial to your climate zone.

In the Landscape

The soft white blooms of flowering dogwood unfold in early spring, followed by light green foliage in April. The flowers are actually bracts, or modified leaves. The true flowers are yellow and are located in the center of the bracts.

The blooms are followed by green berries, but they aren't noticeable until the leaves drop in October and the berries turn glossy red. They don't last long, because birds eat the berries almost as soon as they appear. Fall foliage varies in color from red to reddish purple to orange red.

Planting and Care

In the wild, flowering dogwood is an understory tree, so plant it in partial shade for ideal growth. However, it can tolerate full sun if given adequate water. Avoid hot, dry locations, such as those near parking lots.

No matter what region it grows in, this tree requires rich, acidic, well-drained soil. To reduce soil temperature and to retain soil moisture,

Few trees can bring springtime woods to life like flowering dogwood.

add 3 inches of mulch under the canopy.

Native dogwoods have fallen prey to anthracnose, a disease that causes the tree to lose its leaves. Some fungicides minimize loss. Powdery mildew, a mildewlike mold, can also devastate summer foliage (page 158).

Species and Selections

There are 30 to 40 selections available that differ in flower type, flower color, and leaf color. 'Barton White' has large, white overlapping flowers, and 'Cloud 9' has showy white blooms. 'Cherokee Chief' has reddish flowers, 'Hohman's Gold' sports striking green and chartreuse foliage, and 'Junior Miss' bears pink flowers. Kousa dogwood (page 90),

AT A GLANCE

Plant type: deciduous tree

Features: early-spring flowers, red fall berries

Colors: white or pink blooms

Height: 15 to 25 feet

Light: full sun to partial shade

Soil: acidic, well drained, organic

Water: high during summer months

Problems: anthracnose, powdery mildew

Native: Eastern United States

Range: Zones 5 to 9

Remarks: berries attract birds

C. kousa, has been hybridized with flowering dogwood to resist anthracnose (page 158).

Fortune's Osmanthus

Osmanthus x *fortunei*

Beginning in October and continuing through early November, the fragrance of Fortune's osmanthus sweetly perfumes the air. In the South and on the West Coast, this popular Japanese evergreen is valued for its dense, oval form, fruity-scented flowers, and glossy leaves.

In the Landscape

Fortune's osmanthus grows into a large shrub, reaching a height of 10 to 15 feet.

Its thick evergreen foliage and oval shape make it an excellent choice for a natural screen. The heady fragrance of the small white flowers makes up for their lack of showiness. The hollylike leaves grow up to 4 inches long.

Planting and Care

Although Fortune's osmanthus is a carefree plant, the leaves can be burned by severe winters. Full sun or partial shade is required to maintain a dense growth habit. This shrub prefers moist, fertile soil that is well drained.

Fortune's osmanthus is easily pruned and maintained as a loosely clipped hedge or a formal hedge.

Species and Selections

Fortune's osmanthus combines the best characteristics of the parent plants, holly osmanthus and tea olive. Holly osmanthus (*O. heterophyllus*), gets its name from its holly-shaped evergreen leaves. It has a more upright growth habit than Fortune's osmanthus and does

Fortune's osmanthus can grow tall enough to provide a natural screen (above). The intoxicating scent from its flowers is a fall bonus (right).

not grow as tall.

There are many named selections of holly osmanthus that have different leaves and colors. Among the more common ones are 'Aureomarginatus', which has yellow-bordered leaves, and 'Gulftide,' whose compact form boasts spiny foliage.

The other parent plant, tea olive (*O. fragrans*), produces small, fragrant flowers in the early spring and is less cold tolerant; low temperatures will burn its leaves. Tea olive has long been a favorite landscape screen in the deep South, where it often grows to 20 feet or more. In the North, this plant is a popular container-grown greenhouse plant.

AT A GLANCE

Plant type: evergreen shrub

Features: fragrant fall flowers, glossy leaves, oval growth habit

Colors: white blooms

Height: 10 to 15 feet

Light: full sun to partial shade

Soil: moist, well drained, fertile

Water: medium

Problem: none specific

Native: hybrid origin

Range: Zones 7 to 9

Remarks: makes a good clipped hedge

Glossy Abelia

Abelia x grandiflora

Any blooming evergreen shrub has a sure place on a list of landscape plants. Glossy abelia combines many desirable traits, including evergreen foliage, small white flowers that last from spring to fall, controllable size, tolerance of neglect, and freedom from pests. Glossy abelia is a popular accent plant in gardens from New York to Florida, and prefers temperatures that do not dip too far below zero degrees Fahrenheit.

In the Landscape

Glossy abelia grows 3 to 8 feet tall and can be pruned into a clipped hedge, or left alone to develop a more informal, arching form. Either way, it provides an attractive backdrop for other shrubs or garden perennials.

The lustrous foliage is dark green during the growing season, but it turns bronze in winter. Creamy white tubular-shaped flowers appear in May and June and last until frost.

Planting and Care

Plant glossy abelia in full sun or partial shade. For best results, this plant needs well-drained, slightly acidic soil. Blooming is strongest when plants receive at least six hours of direct sunlight daily. Glossy abelia responds well to periodic pruning, especially older plants that have old, woody growth.

To reduce winter damage, plant glossy abelia where it doesn't receive early morning

Whether pruned into a hedge or left to grow in its freest form, glossy abelia requires little care.

sun and where it is protected from harsh winter winds.

Species and Selections

Many dwarf forms of abelia make good foundation plants and ground covers. 'Prostrata' is a low-growing, compact selection that grows only 3 to 4 feet tall. 'Sherwood', which is more dense and compact, reaches 3 feet at maturity.

'Francis Mason' is known for its unusual golden yellow foliage, while 'Edward Goucher' is valued for pink flowers that appear in June and last until frost.

AT A GLANCE

Plant type: evergreen shrub

Features: glossy foliage; profuse, bell-shaped summer flowers

Colors: white blooms

Height: 3 to 8 feet

Light: full sun to partial shade

Soil: well drained, slightly acidic

Water: medium

Problems: none specific

Native: hybrid origin

Range: Zones 5 to 9

Remarks: tough, drought tolerant

Greek Myrtle

Myrtus communis

Greek myrtle is a classic shrub linked to the Greek goddess of love, Aphrodite. A native of the Mediterranean region, this evergreen shrub grows well in warm, dry landscapes and becomes more treelike as it ages.

In the Landscape

Greek myrtle grows into a wide, rounded evergreen with dark, glossy green foliage. It reaches a height of 10 feet at maturity.

In April, Greek myrtle is covered with prominent stamens. The small, fragrant, white blooms linger for several weeks and are followed by bluish black berries that last for several months.

Greek myrtle is often used in foundation plantings in Florida and Southern California, where the climate is similar to its native habitat. This shrub also makes a good screen, and works well as a container plant.

Planting and Care

Because Greek myrtle tolerates sandy soil, it is often used in coastal landscapes. Although this plant requires little care, for best growth, protect Greek myrtle from direct salt spray. Provide fertile, well-drained, moist soil, and fertilize it in sandy soil. Because it is sensitive to cold, it should only be grown in Zones 9 and higher. Greek myrtle also grows well in filtered shade.

This plant can sometimes

Dark green, glossy foliage is a hallmark of Greek myrtle (right). The showy flowers emit a sweet scent when they bloom in spring (above).

come under attack by scales and mites. To control them, use insecticidal sprays.

Species and Selections

A few selections offer different sizes, leaf shapes, and variegation. 'Compacta' is a slow-growing variety with small, glossy foliage and a tight form. 'Microphylla' has small, lance-shaped leaves, while the green leaves of 'Variegata' are marbled with creamy white.

Related members of the myrtle family include species of bottlebrush, pineapple guava, melaleuca, and strawberry guava. As with Greek myrtle, these species can't tolerate freezing temperatures.

AT A GLANCE

Plant type: evergreen shrub

Features: spring blooms, glossy foliage, open growth habit

Colors: white flowers

Height: 10 feet

Light: full sun to partial shade

Soil: fertile, well drained, moist

Water: low to medium

Problems: scales and mites

Native: Mediterranean region

Range: Zones 9 and higher

Remarks: grows well in filtered shade

Green and Gold

Chrysogonum virginianum

An American native, green and gold is one of the best woodland ground covers in the Eastern United States. Also known as golden star, this perennial produces starlike golden yellow flowers throughout spring and sporadically in early summer. This species grows successfully in Zones 5 to 9, ranging from Southern Ohio and Pennsylvania south to Florida and Mississippi.

In the Landscape

Green and gold grows 6 to 12 inches high, making it a good candidate to highlight the edge of a shady border. Although the sunny flowers get most of the attention, the "toothed" dark green leaves provide a cool contrast in the garden from early spring until fall.

Green and gold makes an exceptional ground cover; unlike most flowering ground covers, it can tolerate shade.

Planting and Care

True to its native habitat, green and gold grows well in partial to full shade. It will, however, tolerate more sun if consistent moisture is available. Provide moist, well-drained, fertile soil for best growth. Green and gold requires little fertilizer and needs additional watering during periods of drought. This plant is self-sowing and seed-

With its sunny flowers and dark foliage, green and gold spreads rapidly across the shady garden.

lings are easy to transplant. However, division is the most reliable method of propagation.

Species and Selections

Green and gold's appearance varies greatly. The Northern variety is taller and more upright than the Southern varieties. Some popular selections for the South include 'Allen Bush', an 8-inch-tall plant, and 'Mark Viette', which grows 6 inches high. 'Picadilly' is an excellent prostrate form. The variety *australe* spreads rapidly, but the flowers are not as showy and fade more rapidly.

AT A GLANCE

Plant type: perennial

Features: star-shaped spring blooms, dark green foliage

Colors: golden yellow flowers

Height: 6 to 12 inches

Light: partial to full shade

Soil: moist, well drained, fertile

Water: low

Problems: none specific

Native: Eastern United States

Range: Zones 5 to 9

Remarks: makes a carefree woodland ground cover

Heavenly Bamboo

Nandina domestica

The canelike stems of heavenly bamboo give this plant its name. Also called nandina, this native of China grows in Zones 6 to 9.

In the Landscape

At maturity, heavenly bamboo can attain a height of 6 to 8 feet and a width of 4 feet by colonizing, or sending new shoots outward from the roots. Heavenly bamboo's layered, evergreen foliage works well for screening, in mass plantings, or as an accent. In winter, several selections take on unusual leaf colors, varying from red to copper to purple.

This shrub's attributes go beyond form and foliage to its most highly valued feature—its fruiting character. In the spring, large clusters of white flowers appear, followed by grapelike clusters of berries that redden in the fall and persist into winter.

Planting and Care

Old specimens of heavenly bamboo have been found in abandoned homesites in the South, demonstrating its hardiness as a landscape shrub.

Heavenly bamboo will grow in full sun to deep shade. It adapts to a variety of soil conditions, but it prefers moist, fertile soil.

To prevent legginess and to encourage berries, prune the oldest canes to encourage new growth, or cut them back at varying heights along existing canes. This can be done any

The narrow leaves of heavenly bamboo (above) give it a feathery texture. Large clusters of red berries contrast with the dark green foliage in the fall (right).

time from late spring to midsummer. Don't wait until later in the year, or the plant may produce late growth that will not harden off before winter.

Species and Selections

Thanks to an abundance of selections, gardeners have a wide range of form, size, leaf color, and texture to choose from. 'Alba' has white fruit, while 'Gulfstream' offers a compact, mounding form with red winter foliage. 'Harbor Dwarf' has a compact growth habit and features purple-tinged winter foliage, and 'San Gabriel' sports fernlike foliage.

AT A GLANCE

Plant type: evergreen shrub

Features: feathery leaf texture, spring blooms followed by fall berries

Colors: white flowers, bright red orange berries

Height: 6 to 8 feet

Light: full sun to deep shade

Soil: moist, fertile soil

Water: medium

Problems: none specific

Native: China

Range: Zones 6 to 9

Remarks: low-maintenance plant

Hinoki False Cypress

Chamaecyparis obtusa

Although not extensively cultivated in America, Hinoki false cypress is an evergreen tree with much to offer. Native to Japan and Taiwan, it grows dependably in Zones 4 to 8. Its loose but stately growth habit makes it a model species for Oriental-style gardens.

In the Landscape

Although the form of Hinoki false cypress varies with the selection, the tree generally grows into a conical shape.

Specimens of the true species can attain a height of 50 to 75 feet with a spread of 10 to 20 feet. Because this plant grows slowly, trees reaching this height are quite old.

The tree's foliage is a flat, clear green, and the markings on the underside of the leaves resemble birds' feet. The dwarf selections are often used in rock and bonsai gardens or as specimen plants.

Planting and Care

Hinoki false cypress grows best in full sun to partial shade. In locations with dense shade, this tree becomes open and leggy. This shrub thrives in well-drained, organic soil and rarely requires pruning.

Hinoki false cypress is usually pest free, but it occasionally suffers from spider mites or juniper scales (see pages 158-159).

Species and Selections

The better selections available at nurseries include 'Crippsii',

Hinoki false cypress is the parent plant of many selections. The dwarf form 'Nana Gracilis' (right) makes a good container plant.

a popular slow-growing dwarf form, which has appealing golden yellow foliage. 'Filicoides' has dense growth and slightly twisted, frondlike branches and bright green foliage. 'Nana' is one of the smallest dwarf forms, growing only 6 inches tall with dark, dull green foliage. 'Nana Gracilis', a dwarf pyramidal form, grows about 4 feet tall, and sports deep lustrous green leaves.

A related species, Japanese false cypress (*C. pisifera*), reaches a towering height of 150 feet, while Atlantic white-cedar, a native of the Eastern United States, grows 75 feet tall. This species tolerates poor soil and grows well in Zones 3 to 8.

AT A GLANCE

Plant type: evergreen tree

Features: conical form

Foliage: green, fernlike sprays

Height: 50 to 75 feet

Light: full sun to partial shade

Soil: well drained, organic soils

Water: low to medium

Problems: spider mites, juniper scales

Native: Japan and Taiwan

Range: Zones 4 to 8

Remarks: dwarf selections work well in containers or Japanese-style gardens

Indian Hawthorn

Raphiolepis umbellata

Gardeners often overlook dwarf plants in favor of larger, more spectacular shrubs and trees that will reach maturity in three or four years. However, low-growing evergreen shrubs such as Indian hawthorn have the advantage of being low maintenance.

Indian hawthorn, which thrives in the warm climates of Zones 8 to 10, blooms in the spring with pinkish white flowers that give way to black fruits that last well into the summer. Its foliage remains glossy green throughout the year but may turn purple in winter.

In the Landscape

Indian hawthorn grows to a mature height of 4 to 6 feet with an equal spread in less than 10 years. Some forms of Indian hawthorn become treelike in character, but the typical form is distinctly rounded.

Because of its tidy growth habit, Indian hawthorn works well in the front of a mixed shrub border. This plant also lends itself to mass plantings and is an apt substitute for Japanese holly.

Planting and Care

For best growth and flowering, plant Indian hawthorn in full sun. Fertile, well-drained soil is preferred. This shrub is often used in coastal environments because of its resistance to heat, humidity, and salt spray. Severe winters can kill Indian hawthorn, so plant it in warm climates. Leaf spot, a disease

Given the right growing conditions, Indian hawthorn forms neat, low-growing, compact mounds of evergreen foliage with white to pink flowers.

which can defoliate plants, can be a problem.

Species and Selections

There are many selections of Indian hawthorn, most of which are selected for their flower color and their resistance to leaf spot.

Monrovia Nursery in California has developed a number of selections, including 'Ballerina', which has bright, rosy pink flowers, and 'Enchantress', a compact form with large pink flowers. 'Indian Princess' features large, bright pink flowers, while 'Snow White' is a dwarf spreading form with white flowers. 'Springtime', a fast-growing selection, has leathery bronze-green foliage and pink flowers.

AT A GLANCE

Plant type: evergreen shrub

Features: spring flowers, mounding growth habit

Colors: glossy green foliage, white to pink blooms, blue berries

Height: 4 to 6 feet

Light: full sun

Soil: fertile, well drained, tolerates sandy soil

Water: medium

Problems: leaf spot

Native: Southern China

Range: Zones 8 to 10

Remarks: tolerates salt spray

Japanese Aucuba

Aucuba japonica

Japanese aucuba has many worthy qualities. The coarse-textured leaves may be its most noticeable feature, but its attributes don't stop there. Adaptability to a variety of soil conditions, tolerance of deep shade, and a remarkable toughness make Japanese aucuba one of the most versatile evergreen shrubs.

In the Landscape

Also known as gold-dust plant, owing to its yellow-speckled, deep green leaves, Japanese aucuba brings an exotic feel to the landscape. Although solid green forms of this plant are available, the variegated selections are more ornamental. This shrub grows to 5 to 10 feet with a similar spread.

Japanese aucuba is a dioecious plant, which means that plants are distinctly male or female. To ensure a crop of red fruit in October and November, female flowers must be fertilized with pollen from a nearby male shrub.

Planting and Care

Japanese aucuba grows best in shade. Direct, overhead sunlight will scorch the leaves. Plant it in moist, organic soil that is well drained; soggy conditions will kill it.

This tough plant requires little care. Few insects and diseases plague it, and pruning is seldom required if the plant is located where it can grow to its natural size.

Although once thought to be cold sensitive, Japanese

Like sunshine in shadow, Japanese aucuba brightens shady garden spots with its yellow-flecked foliage.

aucuba can withstand freezing temperatures in Zones 7 to 10. Severe winters, however, can kill the foliage; occasionally the whole plant will die from exposure to cold.

Although Japanese aucuba is usually a pest-free plant, sclerotinia leaf fungus can cause the leaves to turn black and the stems to die back. Before purchasing plants, check with your county Extension agent to find out if this problem is prevalent in your area.

Propagate Japanese aucuba from softwood cuttings.

Species and Selections

There are many selections that differ in color and leaf shape. 'Crotonifolia' has speckled yellow leaves, while 'Fructo Albo' has white variegated leaves.

'Nana' has a compact growth habit, while 'Picturata' sports solid yellow blotched variegation. 'Variegata', or gold-dust plant, features yellow variegation.

AT A GLANCE

Plant type: evergreen shrub

Features: coarse, glossy leaves; fall fruit

Colors: green foliage with yellow flecks

Height: 5 to 10 feet

Light: partial to deep shade

Soil: well drained, organic

Water: medium

Problems: sclerotinia leaf fungus

Native: Japan

Range: Zones 7 to 10

Remarks: variegated selections available

Japanese Fatsia

Fatsia japonica

Japanese fatsia is one of the most dramatic foliage plants for American gardens. Large, deeply serrated leaves, up to 1 foot in diameter, and a dark green color give the plant its eye-catching appearance.

In the Landscape

Japanese fatsia grows in a dense, round habit; as it ages, it takes on a sculptural character. The plant grows quickly, reaching a height of almost 8 feet with a similar spread in less than 10 years. In late October and November, large clusters of creamy white flowers appear. The blooms are followed by dark black berries that last for 4 to 6 weeks.

Because of its dramatic foliage, Japanese fatsia works well in mass plantings with Japanese aucuba (page 76) and cast-iron plant. It is also a popular container plant because it can tolerate low-light conditions. However, be sure to provide it with several hours of sunlight daily and place it outside during summer.

Planting and Care

Although it grows well in the warm climate of Zones 8 to 10, Japanese fatsia thrives in partial to deep shade. Too much light causes the leathery leaves to burn. This shrub prefers rich, organic soil, although it will grow in clay soil.

To ensure dense growth, look for nursery plants with several healthy young shoots at the tips of the stems. If

A large, irregular planting of Japanese fatsia (above) contrasts with the simple lines of a contemporary house. On closer inspection (right), the leaves are shaped like open palms.

available, select a plant with several stems, since it will produce a more compact, bushier plant. Give the shrub a light pruning every year to keep it from becoming too treelike. Fertilize Japanese fatsia using a general all-purpose fertilizer in late winter or early spring.

Scales and spider mites can be major pests. A severe infestation can kill Japanese fatsia; treat it with a recommended insecticide.

Species and Selections

A few named selections exist, including 'Aurea', which has gold variegated leaves, 'Moseri', a compact form, and 'Variegata', which has white variegated foliage. A related species,

x *Fatshedera lizei*, is a cross between Japanese fatsia, *F. japonica* 'Moseri', and English ivy, *Hedera helix* 'Hibernica'.

AT A GLANCE

Plant type: evergreen shrub

Features: coarse, glossy green foliage; fall flowers

Color: white blooms, dark black seeds

Height: up to 8 feet

Light: partial to deep shade

Soil: moist, organic

Water: medium

Problems: scales, spider mites

Native: Japan

Range: Zones 8 to 10

Remarks: lends tropical effect to landscape

Japanese Pagoda Tree

Sophora japonica

Japanese pagoda tree earned its common name because it was often planted near Buddhist temples in Asia, especially in Japan. A yellow dye can be extracted from this deciduous shade tree by baking the flowers until brown and then boiling them in water.

In the Landscape

A member of the legume or pea family, Japanese pagoda tree blooms in July and August, producing large clusters of yellow pealike flowers. As the flowers fade and fall, petals carpet the ground under the canopy.

While most trees bloom after 10 to 15 years, some gardeners have reported flowering after only three to five years. After blooming, bright green pods appear that eventually turn yellow to brown, before dropping in the fall and winter.

At maturity, Japanese pagoda tree easily reaches a height of 50 to 75 feet with a similar spread. In the first 10 years, it will grow 25 feet. It has a symmetrical form, developing a broadly rounded crown as it ages.

Because it withstands heat and drought once established, this tree is a good choice for cities, locations with poor soil, parks, and golf courses. However, it can be messy because its petals, fruits, leaves, and pods drop at different times throughout the year.

The yellow blooms of Japanese pagoda tree swath its canopy in color (right). The summer blooms are large and long-lasting (above).

Planting and Care

To maximize blooming and growth, plant Japanese pagoda tree in full sun and provide loamy, well-drained, fertile soil. This tree is undaunted by air pollution, drought, pests, or diseases.

Japanese pagoda tree will not grow as well in subtropical and tropical climates as it will in Zones 4 to 8.

Species and Selections

The nursery trade offers many selections of this tree, including 'Regent', a fast-growing plant with an upright growth habit that takes six to eight years to flower. 'Princeton

Upright' has a compact, branching character, while 'Pendula' has a weeping form and rarely flowers. 'Variegata' has white speckled leaves.

AT A GLANCE

Plant type: deciduous tree

Features: late-summer yellow blooms, bright green pods

Height: 50 to 75 feet

Light: full sun

Soil: well drained, fertile, loamy

Water: medium

Problems: none specific

Native: Asia

Range: Zones 4 to 8

Remarks: drought tolerant

Japanese Pieris

Pieris japonica

Resembling a long strand of pearls, the creamy flowers of Japanese pieris, also known as Japanese andromeda, signal the arrival of spring. A relative of mountain laurel (page 102), this shrub, with its evergreen foliage and wandering, unpredictable growth habit, brings an individual style to the garden that defies duplication.

In the Landscape

Japanese pieris has a large, sculptural form, reaching 9 feet or more at maturity, and 4 to 6 feet in width.

The foliage is a glossy dark green and grows in rosettes at the ends of branches. New foliage is often tinged bronze, a characteristic in many selections. Flowers appear in late winter or early spring, followed by flower buds in the summer.

Japanese pieris looks beautiful in a naturalistic setting with rhododendrons or azaleas, and it can brighten a glade of ferns as a specimen plant. The shrub also makes a good accent plant beside an entryway or garden statue.

Planting and Care

Plant Japanese pieris in fertile, slightly acidic, moist, well-drained soil. In colder zones, it will take full sun, but it prefers partial shade. Japanese pieris is easy to grow, but it can suffer from dieback. To minimize damage, provide shelter from winter winds.

This shrub is susceptible to lacebugs, which feed on the

Pearl-like strands of flowers hang from the branches of Japanese pieris (right). The shrub has a spreading growth habit (above).

leaves and eventually destroy them. To control these pests, spray the plant with pesticides according to label directions.

Species and Selections

Selections of Japanese pieris offer a variety of flower color and foliage. 'Christmas Cheer', an early-flowering plant, has pink blooms, while 'Mountain Fire' has bright red new growth and white flowers. 'Pygmaea', a dwarf form, has white flowers, while 'Valley Valentine' sports deep rose-pink flowers and lustrous dark green foliage. 'White Cascade' has unusually long, white flowers.

A related species, mountain pieris (*P. floribunda*), bears

AT A GLANCE

Plant type: evergreen shrub

Features: pearl-like strands of flowers in late winter or early spring

Colors: white blooms

Height: 9 feet

Light: partial shade, full sun in cooler climates

Soil: well drained, fertile, slightly acidic

Water: medium

Problems: lacebugs

Native: Japan

Range: Zones 5 to 8

Remarks: makes a good sculptural accent

fragrant white blooms in mid-spring and grows 2 to 6 feet tall.

Japanese Plum Yew

Cephalotaxus harringtonia

Japanese plum yew is a shrub with an identity crisis. It looks like a yew and has evergreen needles like a juniper. Its popularity has grown, thanks to its appealing horizontal-spreading growth habit, its heat tolerance, and its ability to be transplanted as a container plant.

In the Landscape

Japanese plum yew can grow to look like a small tree, but it is more often used as a wide-spreading, loosely compact shrub. It grows slowly, reaching a height of 4 to 6 feet, with a spread of 5 to 10 feet. Since it grows slowly, it also makes a good foundation plant. Use them singly or in mass.

Japanese plum yew is also a good substitute for juniper. Although it grows more slowly, it has a similar growth habit and can tolerate more shade.

Planting and Care

Japanese plum yew is a care-free plant in the landscape and is not bothered by diseases or pests. Little pruning is needed because it grows slowly and neatly. Just prune upward-growing shoots to maintain the horizontal form.

Plant Japanese plum yew in well-drained, moist soil. For best growth, provide partial shade, although it tolerates full sun. Japanese plum yew is one of the best needle evergreens to use in the shade and heat of the South.

Japanese plum yew is a large shrub that can provide an attractive evergreen screen (above). Use 'Fastigiata' where you would plant juniper (right).

Species and Selections

There are several selections of Japanese plum yew that vary in form and growth habit. 'Duke Gardens', a selection discovered in the gardens of Duke University, has a more compact, dense form than the species. 'Fastigiata', a selection popular in Japanese gardens, has dense black-green needles and grows to a height of 10 feet.

'Nana' and 'Prostrata' are horizontal-spreading, dwarf forms of the species. 'Prostrata', which grows only 2 to 3 feet tall, won the 1994 Pennsylvania Horticultural Society's Gold Medal award.

AT A GLANCE

Plant type: evergreen shrub

Features: horizontal-spreading growth habit, long needles, red fruits

Height: 4 to 6 feet

Light: full sun to partial shade

Soil: well-drained, moist, fertile

Water: low, intolerant of wet soil

Problems: none specific

Native: Japan

Range: Zones 5 to 9

Remarks: requires little care or pruning

Japanese Zelkova

Zelkova serrata

I f you are looking for a shade tree that resembles American elm yet is resistant to Dutch elm disease, Japanese zelkova fits both requirements. This Japanese native is best known for its vase-shaped form and speedy growth, providing shade before it reaches maturity.

In the Landscape

Japanese zelkova grows to a height of 50 to 80 feet with a similar spread. It is important to select a tree with a well-developed branch structure so that as the tree grows, it maintains its characteristic vase-shaped form. The bark is smooth and silvery and resembles the bark of American beech. In autumn, the serrated, ribbed leaves turn deep maroon red (and occasionally yellow) and retain their color for several weeks.

Both male and female flowers occur on the same tree, but at different levels. The upper branches bear the female flowers and have shorter leaves than the lower branches, where the male flowers occur.

Japanese zelkova adapts well to urban conditions, tolerating air pollution and compacted soil. It also transplants easily as a balled-and-burlapped tree or from a container.

Planting and Care

Japanese zelkova needs full sun in order to develop its classic vase-shaped form. It

Alternate oblong leaves cover the shoots of Japanese Zelkova (above). A row of 'Green Vase' trees creates an attractive alleé (right).

prefers moist, deep soil, but adapts to clay and loam. Japanese zelkova tolerates wind and withstands periods of drought once established.

In the Lower South, this tree is subject to heat damage and sunscald on the exposed trunk, which is not shielded by the crown. The bark is also susceptible to damage from lawnmowers or other yard equipment, allowing access to insects. To avoid these problems, wrap the lower part of the trunk with a commercial tree wrap.

Species and Selections

'Village Green' is a cold-hardy selection that has a uniform growth habit, making it a good

AT A GLANCE

Plant Type: deciduous tree

Features: upright, vase-shaped

Height: 50 to 80 feet

Light: full sun

Soil: adapted to wide range of soil types and pH

Water: medium; some degree of drought tolerance

Problems: none specific

Native: Japan

Range: Zones 5 to 8

Remarks: resistant to Dutch elm disease

candidate for a street planting. 'Green Vase' is a vase-shaped plant with upright arching branches that grows twice as fast as 'Village Green'. 'Spring Grove' has dark green foliage and vivid fall color.

Katsura Tree

Cercidiphyllum japonicum

Katsura tree may not be as well-known as other shade trees, but it has several notable characteristics. Its small heart-shaped leaves resemble those of Eastern redbud. In autumn, they turn yellow to apricot-orange and have a caramel scent. Native to Japan and China, Katsura tree grows well in Zones 4 to 8.

In the Landscape

Katsura tree is the largest deciduous shade tree in China, reaching a height of 40 to 60 feet with a 20- to 30-foot spread. New foliage emerges reddish purple and fades to blue-green as it matures.

Because of its size, Katsura tree is often planted in open spaces around corporate offices, college campuses, and golf courses. Once established, it grows quickly, developing a pyramidal, spreading form.

Planting and Care

For best growth, plant Katsura tree in full sun, allowing ample room for growth, and provide moist, well-drained, slightly acidic soil. Container and balled-and-burlapped trees are available from specialty nurseries.

Plant specimens in the early spring before new foliage emerges. Katsura tree is not bothered by pests and requires little care, except for extra watering during periods of drought.

The tree's wood is straight-grained and is used in Japan for its lumber. Katsura tree's

Katsura tree has small heart-shaped leaves that emit a caramel scent in autumn. (above). The deciduous tree brings a majestic feeling to the landscape in any season (right).

only weakness is that multiple trunks form and split with age.

Species and Selections

'Pendula' is a selection with a sweeping form and a mound of gracefully weeping branches. It reaches a height of 15 to 25 feet. A related species, *C. magnificum*, has larger leaves and a smaller growth habit. It has copper leaves in the spring that turn blue-green in the summer and golden in the fall.

AT A GLANCE

Plant type: deciduous tree

Features: small, heart-shaped leaves; broad, pyramidal shape; beautiful fall color

Height: 40 to 60 feet

Light: full sun

Soil: well drained, moist, slightly acidic

Water: medium

Problems: none specific

Native: Japan, China

Range: Zones 4 to 8

Remarks: requires extra water during periods of drought

Kousa Dogwood

Cornus kousa

With its white spring flowers and colorful autumn foliage, Kousa dogwood has many of the same attributes as flowering dogwood (page 60). But this deciduous ornamental tree blooms later in the season and, in some gardens, is a hardier choice than flowering dogwood.

In the Landscape

Kousa dogwood is a small tree with an upright, broad, vase-shaped profile. It grows to a mature height of 20 to 30 feet with an equal spread. The tree bears creamy white bracts that are more elongated and pointed than the rounded bracts of other dogwoods. The blooms unfold in early summer, almost a month after flowering dogwood, and are carried on stems above the glossy green foliage.

Another hallmark of Kousa dogwood is its brilliant scarlet fall foliage. In late September, a fruit the size of a small cherry develops at the end of each long stem. Winter brings a better chance to appreciate the tree's deep mahogany bark. The bark peels back to reveal the light brown inner covering.

This tree is best enjoyed at close range, so plant it beside an entryway, over a terrace, or near a patio.

Planting and Care

Kousa dogwood grows well in partial shade and tolerates full sun better than flowering dogwood. For best growth,

Pointed white petals, or bracts, distinguish the flowers of Kousa dogwood.

provide slightly acidic, well-drained, organic soil. In the South, the leaves may curl and turn brown along the edges during the heat of summer. The tree does not suffer from the pest and disease problems common to flowering dogwood.

Species and Selections

Named selections include 'National', which has large bracts and attractive fruit and 'Summer Stars', a plant with large bracts that last for up to six weeks after blooming begins. 'Aurora', 'Stellar Pink', and 'Celestial' are three of several hybrids developed from flowering dogwood and Kousa dogwood. They bloom after flowering dogwood and before Kousa to fill the gap between their seasons. Specialty nurs-

eries carry many of these new selections. With these hybrids, you can enjoy dogwood blooms for two full months.

AT A GLANCE

Plant type: deciduous tree

Features: late-spring or early-summer flowers, red cherrylike fall fruit, brilliant fall foliage

Height: 20 to 30 feet

Light: full sun to partial shade

Soil: well drained, slightly acidic, organic

Water: medium

Problems: none specific

Native: China, Korea, Japan

Range: Zones 5 to 8

Remarks: requires ample water during drought

Leadwort
Ceratostigma plumbaginoides

Two characteristics make leadwort a valuable ground cover. It has a rambling growth habit, and its deep blue flowers bloom in the summer and linger until frost.

In the Landscape

Leadwort grows 8 to 12 inches high, with a spread of 12 to 18 inches. Its deep blue, phlox-like flowers appear in late summer and last until the first frost, easily blending into many garden color schemes.

As an added bonus, the foliage turns reddish bronze in cooler climates. Leadwort is well suited for the front of a border or a rock garden. It also works well on a bank or as part of a container composition.

Planting and Care

Although many species of this plant do not thrive in colder areas, leadwort grows well in Zones 5 to 9. In more Northern zones, plant leadwort in full sun, but in hotter climates, give it afternoon shade. For best growth, plant this perennial in well-drained, fertile soil. Poorly drained areas can cause dieback. To encourage new growth, prune the plant in early spring.

This perennial is also a good plant for indoor forcing. Using artificial light during long days in winter or spring causes the flowers to develop. Plants that are forced in spring will flower again in late summer if moved outside.

Also known as plumbago or indigo flower, leadwort blooms with a tumble of cobalt blue flowers.

To propagate leadwort, take cuttings in spring after new growth has hardened off, or divide established clumps. This perennial is not as winter hardy in Zones 5 and 6, so be sure to protect the plant from the cold by applying several inches of loose mulch.

Species and Selections

A related species, Chinese plumbago (*C. willmottianum*), has similar blue phloxlike flowers, but a more shrublike form. It will endure the poorest soil conditions and grows best in Zones 8 to 10. Griffin's leadwort, *C. griffithii*, has evergreen leaves with red edges.

AT A GLANCE

Plant type: perennial

Features: blooms from summer to fall, glossy green foliage

Colors: deep blue flowers

Height: 8 to 12 inches

Light: full sun to partial shade

Soil: well drained, fertile

Water: medium

Problems: none specific

Native: China

Range: Zones 5 to 9

Remarks: dieback can occur if overwatered, not winter-hardy in northern climate zones

Lenten Rose

Helleborus orientalis

True to its name, Lenten rose blooms around Lent, from January through April. The freckled flowers of this perennial are a welcome sight in the garden when few other flowers are in bloom.

In the Landscape

Lenten rose produces flowers that range from pure white to deep burgundy, with unusual speckled markings. The leathery, coarse-textured foliage is long-lasting and resembles an outspread hand. In cool areas, flowering can begin in the fall. Be sure to protect the plants if you live in an area that has cold winters but no snow cover. This plant does not grow well in tropical regions.

Use Lenten rose in drifts or large clumps in a woodland garden or shady border. Its cup-shaped, nodding flowers are also effective growing on a slope.

Planting and Care

Lenten rose thrives in a partially shaded location, and it prefers rich, moist, organic soil that is slightly alkaline. To improve growth, fertilize Lenten rose in early spring as new foliage emerges.

This plant often reseeds naturally and mature plants rarely need to be divided. Just leave the clumps in place, and transplant the seedlings in the spring after flowering. Handle the brittle roots carefully to avoid damaging them.

Lenten rose contrasts with early-spring daffodils (above). The cup-shaped flowers nod gracefully (right).

Species and Selections

Christmas rose, *H. niger*, a related species, blooms around Christmas and is not well-adapted to Southern zones. Its seeds are spread by snails, who consume the oil covering the seeds and trail the rest away in their slime.

Bearsfoot hellebore, *H. foetidus*, has intriguing chartreuse flowers that have an unpleasant scent. Like Lenten rose, this species self-sows in the garden. Its leathery leaves resemble a bear's clawed foot, giving the plant its common name.

Although many people consider it deciduous, green hellebore (*H. viridis*) is evergreen.

By January, the leaves are ragged and gardeners may choose to cut them away or allow them to disintegrate.

Live Oak

Quercus virginiana

Although live oak grows rapidly when young, reaching 20 feet in the first 10 years, this evergreen tree takes decades to achieve its signature majestic stature. If you have a mature live oak on your property, consider yourself fortunate.

Native from Virginia to Florida and west to Texas and Mexico, live oak is known for its massive size and longevity. At maturity, live oak reaches a height of 60 to 80 feet and a spread of 60 to 120 feet. A mature tree can live for 200 to 300 years.

The wood of live oak has uncommon strength and durability and can withstand almost any natural calamity.

In the Landscape

The leaves of live oak are 2 to 4 inches long, smooth, and shiny black-green during the growing season. Live oak is considered evergreen because the leaves remain on the tree until new spring growth replaces them.

The stout branches of live oak, often as strong as the trunks of other trees, may arch to the ground and then turn up again in an irregular, horizontal habit. This oak tree produces 1-inch-long acorns in clusters or singly that are eaten by songbirds, wild turkey, quail, squirrels, and deer.

Live oak is a good choice for a gardener with a lot of room and patience. Use it either as an open-lawn specimen or to provide shade for a

An alleé of live oaks (above) looms over a gravel drive, while a large tree offers shade for a front yard (right).

driveway. Just be sure to plant the tree at least 20 feet from any pavement. Otherwise, its spreading roots will buckle the pavement. Live oak is a good choice for coastal landscapes, because it tolerates the harsh effects of salt spray. Under these conditions, the trunk develops a distinctive gnarled and weathered character.

Planting and Care

Live oak tolerates shade but will never attain great stature without full sun. This tree grows best in rich, well-drained soil, but it will tolerate just about any soil.

For best results, transplant small live oak trees, placing them 60 feet apart. Prune young trees during their first few years.

AT A GLANCE

Plant type: evergreen tree

Features: upright form, massive size

Height: 60 to 80 feet

Light: full sun

Soil: moist, acidic

Water: medium

Problems: none specific

Native: Southeastern United States and Mexico

Range: Zones 8 to 10

Remarks: slow growing, but worth the wait

Species and Selections

Another related evergreen species well suited for warmer climates is Japanese evergreen oak, *Q. acuta*. This tree has stout, leathery, oval-shaped leaves with blunt points and does not grow well in limestone soil.

Loquat

Eriobotrya japonica

Loquat is one of the most cold-hardy tropical fruiting trees you can find. Also known as Japanese plum, this versatile plant has an unusually coarse, rugged appearance that contrasts vividly with other plants in the landscape.

In the Landscape

Loquat grows in an upright, broad-spreading fashion, making it a good patio or specimen tree. It also works well as an espalier on sunny walls because its supple branches are easy to train. At maturity, loquat reaches a height of 15 to 25 feet, with a spread of 10 to 15 feet.

The evergreen leaves are dark green on the upper surfaces and gray-green with a brown, wooly fuzziness underneath. In late fall, fragrant, creamy white flowers bloom in clusters on the ends of the branches. Yellow, fleshy edible fruit ripen in late winter and early spring.

Planting and Care

For best flowering and fruiting, loquat needs full sun. Although it tolerates partial shade, the flowers and fruit will not be as abundant. Loquat prefers loamy, organic, slightly acidic soil that is well drained; however, it tolerates sandy, slightly alkaline soil. This tree demands a lot of water during establishment; later, it can withstand moderate drought.

In Zone 8, loquat can be damaged in severe winters, so be sure to protect it during a cold snap.

With its large, leathery leaves, loquat (above) forms a graceful canopy. The fleshy fruit ripens in late winter and early spring (right).

Loquat is susceptible to fire blight, a bacterial disease that kills entire branches, so it is best not to overfertilize. Cut out diseased foliage, sterilizing pruners with alcohol between cuts. To prevent further infestation, avoid growing other plants near loquat that are susceptible to this disease, such as pyracantha or pear trees.

Species and Selections

Several selections have been developed for consistent fruit quality. 'Champagne' has yellow-skinned, fleshy, tart fruit, while 'Golden Nugget' has larger, gold-skinned sweeter fruit. 'MacBeth' bears unusually large, yellow-skinned, fleshy fruit.

AT A GLANCE

Plant type: evergreen tree

Features: late-fall creamy white flowers, late-winter fruit

Height: 15 to 25 feet

Light: full sun to partial shade

Soil: loamy, organic, slightly acidic

Water: high during establishment

Problems: fire blight

Native: China

Range: Zones 8 to 10

Remarks: selections have been bred for superior fruit

For variety in leaf color, try 'Variegata', a plant with white variegated leaves. A related species, bronze loquat, *E. deflexa*, has coppery red new foliage.

Mexican Bush Sage

Salvia leucantha

I n the fall, when most summer flowers are past their prime, the brilliant blooms of Mexican bush sage are in full glory, adding a dash of purple to the fall garden. This salvia is also called velvet sage because its leaves resemble the downy surface of velvet. This plant is not perennial north of Zone 8 but, if it is grown as an annual, it will reach its full size.

In the Landscape

Mexican bush sage grows rapidly after plants are set out in late spring. A single-stemmed transplant set in the garden will reward you with a vase-shaped plant 4 feet tall and equally wide by the time it blooms in September. Its fuzzy flowers are a bright purple and appear atop 15- to 20-inch spikes.

Plant Mexican bush sage in the back of a border, or use it as an accent plant. Many garden varieties of chrysanthemums blend well with this plant.

Planting and Care

For best flowering and growth, plant Mexican bush sage in full sun in fertile, well-drained soil. Although it tolerates drought, this plant needs adequate water to fuel rapid growth. To prevent flower stalks from flopping over and to reduce staking, pinch the plant during the growing season.

Mexican bush sage makes an excellent cut flower; hang bouquets upside down in a

The bright purple spikes of Mexican bush sage mix well with a sunny border of yellow garden mums and Mexican heather (right).

dark, cool place, such as a basement, so they will dry without losing their color.

Species and Selections

Other late-summer and fall-blooming salvias include pineapple sage (*S. elegans*), a plant with red flowers and foliage that smells like pineapple when it is crushed. Forsythia sage (*S. madrensis*) is pale yellow, while autumn sage (*S. greggii*) has flowers that range in color from magenta to red and coral to white. Anise sage (*S. guaranitica*) has the largest flowers of all salvias, ranging in color from deep blue to dark lavender. Its foliage has a faint spicy scent.

AT A GLANCE

Plant type: perennial

Features: fall blooms on long spikes, thin leaves

Colors: purple flowers with white inner petals

Height: 3 to 4 feet

Light: full sun

Soil: well-drained, fertile

Water: medium during summer

Problems: none specific

Native: Mexico

Range: Zone 8

Remarks: grown as an annual in more Northern climates

Mountain Laurel

Kalmia latifolia

In the language of flowers, mountain laurel is said to symbolize ambition, an apt word to describe this plant. A beautiful shrub in any season, mountain laurel explodes into bloom in late spring or early summer to light up the shade with masses of bell-shaped blossoms.

The inch-wide, five-sided flowers emerge light pink from deep pink buds and open to reveal burgundy markings dappled around the inside. This native American shrub grows from Maine to Northern Florida and west to Louisiana.

In the Landscape

For all its positive qualities, this flowering evergreen has only one drawback—it grows slowly. Its slow growth rate contributes to its irregular form and sculptural nature. As a young shrub, its form is compact and dense, but with maturity, it transforms into an almost treelike plant.

Locate mountain laurel in a spot where you will not have to prune it—it should not be cut except to remove dead or damaged wood. However, to encourage more blooms, you may snip off spent flower heads.

Planting and Care

In its native habitat, mountain laurel is found growing along creek banks in deep shade. For this plant to thrive in your garden, give it acidic, moist, well-drained soil. During the summer months, keep plants mulched, preferably with

Mountain laurel is well-suited for a low-maintenance garden, where shrubs are allowed to reach their natural form and size.

shredded leaves. Although it thrives in a shady setting, mountain laurel has a high tolerance for direct sun, which will increase blooming. Just be sure it receives adequate water.

This shrub is susceptible to leaf spot, which may disfigure the foliage and cause the leaves to drop. If you see spots on the foliage, contact your local Extension agent for a recommended method of control.

Species and Selections

There are more than 50 different selections of this species that vary widely in appearance. 'Alba' has pure white flowers, while 'Myrtifolia' is a compact form that remains under 6 feet tall. 'Pink Charm'

has red flower buds that are rich pink when they first open, and 'Rubra' has deep pink flowers. The blooms of 'Shooting Star' have deeply cut, reflexed lobes.

New England Aster
Aster novae-angliae

New England aster offers a riot of color in late summer and early fall. Aster, which is Latin for star, describes the starlike shape of its blooms. More than 60 species of aster are native to the Eastern United States from New England to Alabama.

In the Landscape

Selections of New England aster grow 3 to 5 feet tall. While most bloom in shades of purple in September and October, this species may also sport red or pink flowers with yellow centers. This perennial grows quickly and is easily cultivated. Because of its height, New England aster works well in the middle to the back of a fall flower border.

Planting and Care

Although New England aster thrives in almost any garden setting, for best growth, plant it in full sun in well-drained, fertile soil. Since this plant grows tall, it requires staking to prevent the blooms from flopping over.

Pinch New England aster to keep it bushy and upright. In the Northeast, shear the taller variety around July 4; in the South, pinch the plant in early summer, but no later than early July. When planting these perennials in a border, allow plenty of space for growth. As clumps mature, divide them every two to three years during the spring.

Powdery mildew, a disease that looks like a white, feltlike

In early autumn, New England aster is covered with soft purple blooms (above). This 3- to 5-foot-tall perennial brings dimension to a flower border (right).

coating on the surface of leaves, can be a problem in high humidity. Apply a fungicidal application of sulfur dust or spray.

Species and Selections

New York aster, *Aster novi-belgii,* is a related species. Also called Michelmas daisy, this plant grows 3 to 4 feet tall and bears blue-violet blooms. Many named selections exist, including 'Barr's Pink', which has rose-pink, semidouble flowers. Others include 'Mt. Everest', which has white flowers, and 'Purple Dome', which has purple flowers. 'Harrington's Pink' has 2-inch-wide salmon-pink flowers and blooms in midsummer.

AT A GLANCE

Plant type: perennial

Features: daisylike fall flowers

Colors: purple, pink, or red blooms

Height: 3 to 5 feet

Light: full sun

Soil: well drained, moderately fertile

Water: medium

Problems: powdery mildew

Native: Eastern United States

Range: Zones 4 to 8

Remarks: requires staking

Oakleaf Hydrangea
Hydrangea quercifolia

With its huge balls of paperlike flowers, hydrangeas are a refreshing and dependable old-fashioned favorite. None is more spectacular than the flowers of oakleaf hydrangea. This attractive shrub is native to the rolling hills of North Georgia and Alabama, and can be grown in every region of the South except Southern Florida.

In the Landscape

Oakleaf hydrangea gets its common name from its large, coarse leaves that resemble the leaves of an oak tree. At maturity, this shrub can reach a height of 6 to 8 feet with an equal spread. Often the roots will extend to create great tangled colonies of shrubs.

When in bloom, the large white flowers almost cover the plant. A single cluster may be as long as 1 foot. During the hottest part of summer, the flowers are creamy white; but as the weather starts to cool, they begin to turn pink and eventually deepen to red. In late autumn, as the flowers die, the petals turn parchment brown.

The flowers are followed by brilliant autumn foliage that ranges from brownish red to scarlet. When the leaves are gone, the shrub reveals its twisting stems and attractive peeling bark.

Use oakleaf hydrangea in mass, spacing them at least 8 feet apart to create a sweeping border. This shrub mixes well with rhododendron and moun-

Large white flower clusters cover oakleaf hydrangea in early summer (above). Fall flushes the shrub's deeply lobed leaves with burgundy (right).

tain laurel (page 102). To play up its papery flower clusters, plant oakleaf hydrangea in front of an evergreen background.

Planting and Care

Since oakleaf hydrangea is an understory shrub, it thrives in partial shade. However, if it is protected from the heat of the afternoon sun, it will do well in full sun, too.

Plant oakleaf hydrangea in moist, organic, well-drained soil. Without adequate moisture, this plant's leaves will wilt quickly, particularly when in full bloom.

Species and Selections

There are few named selections of oakleaf hydrangea.

AT A GLANCE

Plant type: deciduous shrub

Features: large white flowers; fall color, peeling bark

Height: 4 to 8 feet

Light: partial shade, full sun in mountains

Soil: rich, well drained, slightly acidic

Water: low

Problems: none specific

Native: Southeastern United States

Range: Zones 5 to 9

Remarks: dried flower clusters work well in arrangements

'Snowflake' is prized for flower clusters that can grow up to 1½ feet long. 'PeeWee' is a compact form, and 'Snow Queen' has large white flowers and burgundy leaves in fall.

Purple Coneflower

Echinacea purpurea

Whether growing wild along a roadside or standing like sentinels over the garden, purple coneflower attracts attention. Often used for medicinal purposes, especially to ward off a cold, this wildflower grows from Ohio to Iowa, and as far south as Georgia and Mississippi.

In the Landscape

Plant purple coneflower in a large group to create a mass of color along the outer edge of a wooded area or in clumps in sunny parts of a naturalistic landscape.

Because it can grow up to 3 feet high, purple coneflower is a good choice for the middle to the back of a flower border. Combine its bold, pinkish purple flowers with other bright-colored perennials, such as crocosmia (page 54) and butterfly weed (page 38). This species is also a favorite of butterflies and goldfinches, who love their plentiful seed.

Planting and Care

For maximum flowering, plant purple coneflower in full sun, although it tolerates partial shade in the deep South. In its native habitat, this perennial grows in alkaline soil and can benefit from the addition of limestone to acidic soil. It should be well-watered during times of drought and does not require fertilization.

Gardeners often leave dried flower heads on the plant during the winter because they look attractive.

The blooms of purple coneflower rest like parasols atop strong, tall stems (above). The prominent cone in the center of each bloom gives the plant its name (right).

Species and Selections

Selections include 'Bright Star', which has lavender-red blossoms with orange-bronze centers, and 'Crimson Star', which has crimson-red flowers. 'Robert Bloom' has rich red-purple flowers with orange centers. 'White Lustre' and 'White Swan' are 3-foot-tall plants that bear white flowers with greenish bronze centers. Tennessee coneflower, *E. tennesseensis*, an endangered species, is being propagated by specialty nurseries. It has dark mauve flowers with greenish pink centers and blooms from June until August.

AT A GLANCE

Plant type: perennial

Features: tall, brightly colored blooms

Colors: lavender flowers with orange centers

Height: 2 to 3 feet

Light: full sun to partial shade

Soil: alkaline, moderate fertility

Water: medium

Problems: none specific

Native: Southeastern United States

Range: Zones 3 to 10

Remarks: attracts goldfinches, good cut flower, withstands heat

Red Maple

Acer rubrum

The color red defines almost every season for red maple. This native American tree's fall color blazes scarlet. In early spring, beautiful red flowers appear in dense clusters, followed by ruddy fruits with winglike projections. When the leaves emerge, they are often tinged with red before turning dark green in summer.

This deciduous tree grows throughout the Eastern United States from Canada to Florida and as far west as Oklahoma and Texas.

In the Landscape

Red maple is a medium-sized tree that grows to a mature height of 40 to 60 feet with an equal spread. Because of its rapid, rounded growth habit, red maple is the consummate shade tree. Some of the more beautiful graceful forms of red maple grow alongside lakes.

Use this tree in a formal shade planting in front of the house, or as an informal planting along one side of the garden. Red maple is a natural choice along the edge of the driveway or as the main shade tree on a treeless lot.

Planting and Care

Since red maple occurs naturally in low, wet conditions, it grows best in slightly acidic soil that is consistently moist. The best time to plant this tree is in late fall or early winter. Doing so allows its root system to become established before the foliage appears in

Red maple is a beautiful tree in any season. Red fruit hang from the tree in spring (above), while early-autumn foliage is scarlet (right).

spring. Red maple needs a lot of water during the summer months for the first few years after planting. You can purchase it as a container tree or as a balled-and-burlapped tree.

Species and Selections

For reliable fall color, plant a named selection. Some of the more showy choices are 'October Glory' and 'Red Sunset', which have orange to red fall color.

Selections with an upright form include 'Armstrong', 'Celebration', and 'Columnare'. Other species of maples that make good shade trees include Norway maple, *A. plantanoides*, silver maple, *A. saccharinum*, and sugar maple, *A. saccharum*.

AT A GLANCE

Plant type: deciduous tree

Features: red flowers in late winter and early spring, silver-gray bark in winter

Height: 40 to 60 feet

Light: full sun to partial shade

Soil: moist, slightly acidic

Water: high during summer after transplanting

Problems: none specific

Native: Eastern United States

Range: Zones 3 to 9

Remarks: rapid growth, trouble free

River Birch

Betula nigra

The natural versatility of river birch has taken it beyond its native home along streams and lowlands of the Eastern United States and into gardens of all elevations.

A fast-growing tree, river birch thrives in wet or dry soil. Because of its speedy growth and easy culture, it has become a landscape staple.

In the Landscape

River birch is a tree for gardeners with lots of room. It easily grows to a height of 25 to 30 feet in 10 years. A mature tree can reach 40 to 70 feet tall, with an equal spread.

River birch delivers light, airy shade and features shaggy, multicolored bark and an upright growth habit. Lacking showy flowers or fall color, the tree relies on its bark for landscape appeal. In winter, beige paperlike sheets peel back to reveal darker layers of bark.

Because it grows quickly, river birch is often used to shade golf courses, college campuses, and corporate landscapes.

When planting this tree near a house, be sure to place it at least 20 feet from the foundation to permit healthy root development. For the same reason, allow plenty of room for growth if you use river birch around a paved area; the developing roots could crack the pavement.

Planting and Care

River birch is available from nurseries as a container plant

Rapid growth, multicolored bark, and a multistemmed growth habit are all reasons to plant river birch as a front-yard shade tree.

or as a balled-and-burlapped tree.

The best planting time for large birch is the fall or early spring, before the foliage appears.

River birch grows best in full sun to partial shade and prefers moist, slightly acidic soil. However, it will tolerate drier soil. Water the tree during periods of drought, and it will reward you with 3 feet of growth every year.

Pruning should be delayed until summer. In the spring, exposed cut limbs can bleed sap.

Aphids are the primary pest for river birch. If they are present, the area under the tree will be sprinkled with a sticky secretion known as honeydew.

AT A GLANCE

Plant type: deciduous tree

Features: shaggy, multicolored bark; upright growth habit

Height: 40 to 70 feet

Light: full sun

Soil: poor to average

Water: medium

Problems: aphids

Native: Eastern United States

Range: Zones 4 to 9

Remarks: best birch for the South

Insecticidal sprays will control aphid infestations.

Species and Selections

'Heritage' river birch is a selection valued for its light-colored, peeling bark and large, dark green leathery leaves.

Russian Sage

Perovskia atriplicifolia

Russian sage is a member of the mint family, and although it is a native of Tibet, it grows well in Texas and the Gulf South. Like most plants in this family, the crushed foliage of Russian sage has a pungent scent. The silvery gray fernlike foliage of this plant is a striking addition to a flower border.

In the Landscape

Russian sage grows 3 to 4 feet high and equally wide. This perennial grows quickly, so it should be given plenty of room. In mid- to late-summer, Russian sage bears delicate spikes of lavender-blue flowers. Its silvery gray foliage harmonizes well with most plants, making a good background plant for a flower border.

Planting and Care

Russian sage requires little attention, but for best growth, plant it in full sun in well-drained soil. To encourage new growth in the spring, cut the plant back at the end of the growing season. Propagate new plants by offshoots, which occasionally arise after two to three years, or root softwood cuttings—a cutting taken from new wood or tissue that is beginning to harden—in early summer.

Species and Selections

Although the straight species is sold in most garden centers, other selections that differ in leaf type and flower color are available from specialty cata-

The silver-gray leaves of Russian sage underscore feathery wands of lavender flowers.

logs. 'Blue Haze' has pale blue flowers, while 'Blue Spire' has finely dissected leaves and deep violet flowers. 'Blue Mist' has lighter blue flowers than the species and blooms earlier in the season.

Although not as desirable as Russian sage, Caspian perovskia, *P. scabiosifolia*, is a related species that is taller and has darker blue flowers. The foliage is finely cut and has more of a gray-green cast than the gray-white foliage of Russian sage.

AT A GLANCE

Plant type: perennial

Features: silvery gray fernlike foliage, late-summer blooms

Colors: lavender-blue flowers

Height: 3 to 4 feet

Light: full sun

Soil: well drained

Water: medium during summer months

Problems: none specific

Native: Tibet

Range: Zones 5 to 9

Remarks: vigorous growth habit

Small-flowered Alumroot

Heuchera micrantha

Small-flowered alumroot is a shade-loving, evergreen perennial native to Western North America. This species is often called coralbells because its mounded foliage is topped with slender stems of small, bell-shaped flowers.

In the Landscape

This native perennial grows to a height of 1 to 2 feet and is valued for its distinctive ivy-like foliage. In late spring or early summer, showy spikes of creamy white flowers appear.

Use small-flowered alumroot to edge a woodland garden, or plant it in drifts as a ground cover. More colorful selections make great accents in a shaded border.

Planting and Care

For more luxurious foliage, plant small-flowered alumroot in well-drained, moist, organic soil. Because of its shallow root system, this perennial should be mulched or fertilized with organic matter. In warmer climates, it prefers partial shade, although many of the more colorful foliages tolerate additional sunlight.

To propagate this perennial, divide old, established clumps every four to five years in early spring. Where winters are mild, divide them in early spring or fall. You can also sow seeds in spring.

Species and Selections

'Palace Purple' is a selection that has unusual greenish pur-

The variegated foliage of small-flowered alumroot 'Palace Purple' is an incentive to plant it as a ground cover.

ple to deep purple foliage. It won the 1991 Perennial Plant Association Plant of the Year award. 'Bressingham Bronze' has crinkled bronze-purple foliage, while 'Montrose Ruby' has dark purple leaves with silver mottling. 'Ruffles' is named for its ruffled leaves.

Another native species is American alumroot, *H. americana*, which has attractive evergreen foliage. The best selection is 'Sunset', a plant that features purple veins on its leaves.

Another related species, *H. sanguinea*, also known as coralbells, has been interbred extensively by European gardeners. 'Bressingham Blaze' has coral, red, and pink flowers, while 'Mt. St. Helens' has

brick red flowers. 'Chatterbox' grows 19 inches tall and has deep pink flowers, while 'June Bride' grows 15 inches tall and bears white flowers.

AT A GLANCE

Plant type: perennial

Features: variegated foliage; small bell-shaped flowers

Colors: creamy white to pink flower spikes

Height: 18 to 24 inches

Light: partial to full shade

Soil: well drained, organic

Water: medium

Problems: none specific

Native: Western North America

Range: Zones 4 to 8

Remarks: makes a good woodland ground cover

Smooth Hydrangea

Hydrangea arborescens

In much of the South, it would not seem like summer without the graceful white flowers of smooth hydrangea waving gently in the breeze. This deciduous shrub is native to woodlands in the Eastern United States from New York to Iowa and south to Florida and Louisiana.

In the Landscape

Smooth hydrangea is a large, wandering plant that grows quickly, easily reaching a height and spread of 3 to 5 feet in one growing season. This shrub produces suckers from the roots, so plants are dense in form.

As with most hydrangeas, smooth hydrangea is grown for its profuse white flowers, which appear in late June. The blooms are initially pale green but quickly change to white. Large flowers require staking to prevent them from flopping over. As they fade, the blooms turn brown. If cut back early enough, a second flowering is possible in warmer climates.

Plant smooth hydrangea with English ivy, mondo grass, and other low-growing ground covers. The bare winter stems of the shrub offer a striking contrast against the dark green foliage of ground covers. It also grows well on rocky slopes and bluffs.

Planting and Care

Smooth hydrangea requires little care, but it can suffer from powdery mildew, scales, and spider mites. To combat

Smooth hydrangea thrives in shade and well-drained soil.

these problems, spray the shrub with an insecticide.

For best growth, plant smooth hydrangea in well-drained, moist, organic soil. For more profuse flowers, locate the plant in partial shade. However, it will grow in full sun if given adequate moisture. To improve the shrub's looks and health, cut back plants at ground level in late fall or early winter.

Species and Selections

'Annabelle' is a selection that produces flower clusters up to 10 inches wide. 'Grandiflora' produces an even greater show, bearing flower clusters up to 18 inches wide. Bigleaf hydrangea (*H. macrophylla*), another popular species, includes many selections that range in color from pink to blue. It can grow as tall as 10

feet with a spread greater than its height.

AT A GLANCE

Plant type: deciduous shrub

Features: large blooms in midsummer, bright green leaves, rambling growth habit

Colors: white flowers

Height: 3 to 5 feet

Light: full sun to partial shade

Soil: well drained, moist

Water: medium in full sun to prevent wilting

Problems: powdery mildew, scales, spider mites

Native: Eastern United States

Range: Zones 3 to 9

Remarks: staking required for large flower heads

Sourwood

Oxydendrum arboreum

Few native trees brighten summer with the flair of sourwood. Found on upland ridges in the forests of Southern states, this slow-growing, small tree has glorious fall color. If you're looking for a tree to fill a tight space, sourwood is a good bet.

In the Landscape

Sourwood can reach a height of 40 to 60 feet, but more often, it grows 30 to 35 feet tall. This plant is also called lily-of-the-valley tree for the bell-shaped, creamy white flowers it bears in June.

The flowers are followed by fruit that lingers until winter. The leaves of sourwood are dark green and hang in a weeping fashion. One of the first trees to change colors in fall, its foliage turns red to purple.

Sourwood grows unpredictably. Each tree is a tangle of deeply fissured bark and reddish winter twigs. Even when planted in uniform sunlight, sourwood branches randomly, developing an upright character.

Use sourwood as an accent at the edge of a patio or beside a sidewalk. It's also a good low-maintenance tree because it does not require a lot of cleaning up around it.

Planting and Care

For sourwood to reach its full height, plant it in acidic, well-drained, organic soil. During periods of drought give the tree extra water. It grows well in full sun or partial shade,

Sourwood is one of the first trees to show its fall color (right). The tree stretches out thin branches, which appear like graceful fingers dangling in the breeze (above).

although fall color will not be as brilliant in shady locations.

Sourwood is difficult to transplant; full-grown trees go into shock if transplanted. Small, container-grown seedlings have a better chance of survival than larger ones.

Sourwood is attacked by webworm in late summer and early fall. Heavy infestations can cause the tree to lose its leaves. To limit the damage, remove the webs.

Species and Selections

Sourwood is new to the nursery trade, so few selections exist.

'Chameleon' has white, bell-shaped flower clusters

that bloom in late summer. Fall color ranges from red to yellow to lime green.

AT A GLANCE

Plant type: deciduous tree

Features: white flowers in late summer, early-fall color

Height: 25 to 40 feet

Light: full sun to partial shade

Soil: well drained, organic, slightly acidic

Water: medium

Problems: webworm

Native: Southeastern United States

Range: Zones 5 to 9

Remarks: requires extra water during periods of drought to maintain vigor

Southern Magnolia

Magnolia grandiflora

To most people, the word magnolia conjures up an evergreen tree with large, fragrant white flowers. That image is what makes Southern magnolia one of the best-loved ornamental trees in the South.

In the Landscape

Southern magnolia is a slow-growing tree that reaches a height of 60 to 90 feet with a spread of 30 to 40 feet. Everything about this tree is big, so be sure to provide enough space for the plant to grow and mature.

The leaves, which are 5 to 8 inches long, are a glossy deep green and are often used in holiday decorations. Creamy white, fragrant flowers appear in late April and May and sporadically in the summer. In early fall, light green conelike fruits split open to reveal attractive red seeds.

Southern magnolia is large enough to fill distant corners or block unsightly views. It is also a good choice for a beach planting. Its dense foliage will block wind and salt spray all year long, especially when planted in groups of five or more.

Planting and Care

Plant Southern magnolia in either full sun or partial shade, depending on soil conditions. In moist, peaty soil, the tree can tolerate the hot summer sun. In areas where rainfall is irregular or the soil is too light to retain moisture naturally, plant Southern magnolia in

The waxy white flowers of Southern magnolia bloom in contrast to the glossy, deep green foliage.

partial shade, protecting it from the hot afternoon sun.

Southern magnolia requires little care and has no serious pests or diseases. The fallen leaves can be a chore to rake, but if the tree's lower limbs are not pruned away, dropped leaves will be hidden by the interior foliage.

Species and Selections

'Bracken's Brown Beauty' is a compact selection that has rusty brown coloration underneath the leaves. 'Claudia Wannamaker' has dark green foliage, while 'Little Gem' is a compact form with attractive foliage and superior flowers. Other native American magnolias include the semievergreen sweet bay magnolia (page 122), *M. virginiana*, and deciduous species, such as

bigleaf magnolia, *M. macrophylla*, cucumber magnolia, *M. acuminata*, and umbrella magnolia, *M. tripetala*.

AT A GLANCE

Plant type: evergreen tree

Features: large, white fragrant flowers; glossy green foliage

Height: 60 to 80 feet

Light: full sun to partial shade

Soil: organic, slightly acidic, well drained

Water: medium

Problems: none specific

Native: Southeastern United States

Range: Zones 7 to 10

Remarks: makes an effective screen when several are grown together

Spanish Bluebell

Endymion hispanicus

Spanish bluebell brings a bundle of blue flowers to the shade garden in spring. Also known as wood hyacinth, this plant features bell-shaped blooms lifted on slender stalks above glossy green foliage. The flowers hang in pastel clusters, bowing their heads toward the earth.

In the Landscape

To appreciate the burst of color in spring, plant these bulbs in large drifts. They also work well with ground covers, such as ferns and hostas, which help hide the foliage of spent flowers. Since Spanish bluebell prefers shady locations, it is an excellent choice for a woodland garden. This perennial blooms with azaleas and blends with a wide range of colors. Because this plant makes an excellent cut flower, consider adding the bulbs to a cutting garden.

But however beautiful, bluebells are brief; in a few weeks, the foliage dies and all signs of the plant disappear until the next spring.

Planting and Care

Plant bulbs in the fall 2 to 4 inches deep in well-drained soil that receives morning sun. Be sure to add a slow-release bulb fertilizer when planting. In Southern climates, plant bulbs after the soil has cooled but before the first extended frost. Spanish bluebell multiplies quickly and must be divided every three to four years.

The nodding flowers of Spanish bluebell are short-lived (above), but the effect of a field of flowers is long lasting (right).

Species and Selections

'Blue Giant' is a selection with deep blue flowers on 18-inch stems, while 'Dainty Maid' offers rosy pink flowers, and 'White Triumphator' yields clear white flowers. Heirloom varieties include 'Excelsior', which has deep violet-blue flowers, and 'Rose Queen', which has pink flowers.

A related species, English bluebell, (*Hyacinthoides nonscripta*), is often planted in large drifts in English woodlands. This species thrives in Zones 5 to 8.

AT A GLANCE

Plant Type: perennial (bulb)

Features: 20-inch spikes of bell-shaped flowers in spring

Colors: blue, pink, or white blooms

Height: 20 inches

Light: full sun to partial shade

Soil: well drained, acidic

Water: medium

Problems: will rot if overwatered

Native: Spain, Portugal

Range: Zones 4 to 8

Remarks: most effective when planted in large drifts

Spike Gayfeather

Liatris spicata

With its striking resemblance to a feathery bottle brush, spike gayfeather stands guard over the back of a flower border. Unlike most flowers, this plant blooms from top to bottom. Native to Eastern North America, this perennial is often used by florists in cut and dried flower arrangements.

In the Landscape

When spike gayfeather blooms, it can reach a height of 3 to 4 feet. Occasionally, it grows as tall as 5 feet. Its spikes are purple or rose and can be 6 to 15 inches tall. The foliage is narrow and tapered, creating a fine texture. Because of its tall, erect form and simple beauty, spike gayfeather makes a fine border plant.

Planting and Care

For best results, plant spike gayfeather in well-drained, moderately fertile soil. To keep the bulbs from rotting in winter, make sure the soil is well drained. To maximize flowering, plant spike gayfeather in full sun, although it tolerates partial shade. Place bulbs 18 inches apart in groups of five to seven.

Because of its height, this plant may require staking to keep the flower spikes upright. To rejuvenate the plant, divide clumps every three to four years. Bulbs and container plants are available at specialty nurseries.

When planted in the back of a flower border, the stems of spike gayfeather add height to the garden.

Species and Selections

'Kobold', the most common selection, has a compact form, growing only 2 feet tall and producing multiple spikes of lavender flowers. 'Floristan White' has white flowers, while 'Floristan Violet' has violet blooms, and 'August Glory' bears purple-blue flowers.

Related species include pink-scale gayfeather (*L. elegans*), tall gayfeather (*L. scariosa*), and Kansas gayfeather, (*L. pycnostachya*). Pink-scale gayfeather has narrow leaves and purple flower heads, while tall gayfeather has dry, scaly, oblong leaves, and a long cluster of purple flower heads. Leaves crowd the purple flowers of Kansas gayfeather.

AT A GLANCE

Plant type: perennial (bulb)

Features: 3- to 4-inch tall flower spikes, fine-textured foliage

Colors: purple or rose flowers

Height: 3 to 4 feet at flowering

Light: full sun to partial shade

Soil: well drained, moderately fertile

Water: low

Problems: none specific

Native: Eastern North America

Range: Zones 3 to 9

Remarks: excellent cut flower

Stonecrop

Sedum x 'Autumn Joy'

A rugged, durable plant, stonecrop is tailor-made for gardeners who are long on intentions but short on time.

Also known as sedum, this late-blooming perennial emerges in spring with succulent rosettes of leaves that grow into lush mounds of gray-green foliage. By midsummer, beaded tufts of flower buds appear. In fall, the color show begins as the buds open, forming large starlike clusters of pink, rose, crimson, or copper.

In the Landscape

Stonecrop combines nicely with shrubs and other perennials and makes a first-rate edging plant. Plant it with yellow mums, ornamental grasses, coneflowers (page 108), or asters (pages 104 and 136). Mix stonecrop with other plants bearing gray-green foliage, such as lamb's-ears or 'Silver Mound' artemisia.

Planting and Care

Stonecrop enjoys full sun, but it also grows in light shade; however, plants that receive shade may need light pruning in early summer to prevent them from becoming too leggy. The soil must be well drained, or the fleshy stems and leaves will rot. Watering requirements are low except during severe drought.

Set out transplants or divisions in the fall or in early spring. It is important not to mulch stonecrop, because it can cause the plant to rot.

To propagate, snip off a

Stonecrop combines well with ornamental grasses and fall flowers (above). In the autumn, stonecrop turns from pink to coppery red (right).

stem, plant it in moist soil, and watch it take root. Stonecrop also makes an excellent container plant.

Species and Selections

There are many selections of a related species, *S. spectabile*, that are beautiful garden ornamentals. A popular selection called 'Brilliant' has raspberry-red flowers, while 'Carmen' sports rose-pink flowers, and 'Star Dust' is ivory with occasional pink flowers. 'Indian Chief' blooms with copper flowers that turn brick red as they age.

A good variegated choice is 'Variegatum', which has bright pink flowers with yellow variegated foliage.

AT A GLANCE

Plant type: perennial

Features: succulent rosette-like leaves, striking fall blooms

Colors: pink, red, bronze flowers

Height: 12 to 24 inches

Light: full sun to partial shade

Soil: well drained, fertile

Water: low

Problems: none specific

Native: hybrid origin

Range: Zones 3 to 9

Remarks: easy to grow, long-lived

Summersweet

Clethra alnifolia

There's no mystery to summersweet's name. In midsummer, spicy-scented pink or white flowers offset the plant's glossy green leaves. This deciduous shrub was once known as Sailor's Delight, because its fragrance could be detected by those at sea. Summersweet is native from Maine to Florida and east to Texas.

In the Landscape

Summersweet has an upright, oval growth habit. At maturity, specimens can be quite large, sometimes growing as tall as 6 feet or more with a spread of 4 to 6 feet.

The shrub is valued for its spikes of fragrant flowers that appear on new growth in July and August. Fall color varies, but under the most favorable conditions, the leaves turn yellow to golden brown. Summersweet can be used in the landscape as a clipped hedge without much maintenance. It also makes a good seashore plant because it thrives in wet conditions.

Planting and Care

To produce the greatest flower show and to maintain a dense growth habit, plant summersweet in full sun to partial shade. Although this shrub grows naturally in wet conditions, it prefers rich, slightly moist soil.

For maximum flowering, prune summersweet in early spring before new growth appears. Dried flower heads

The white blooms of summersweet (right) yield a spicy scent. In the fall, its green leaves turn golden yellow (above).

should be removed to maintain a tidy appearance.

Species and Selections

Although this shrub's flowers are usually white, there are many selections with different flower colors and sizes.

Many pink selections have distinct rose-pink buds that open to reveal a pale pink or white flower. 'Paniculata' has larger flowers than summersweet, while 'Rosea' has showy pinkish white flowers. 'Pink Spire' has deep pink buds that open to soft pink flowers. 'Hummingbird' is a dwarf form that grows only 4 feet tall and bears abundant white flowers.

A related species, cinnamon clethra, *C. acuminata,*

AT A GLANCE

Plant type: deciduous shrub

Features: spikes of fragrant flowers in summer, yellow to golden brown fall foliage

Colors: white to pink blooms

Height: 6 to 8 feet

Light: full sun to partial shade

Soil: organic, slightly moist

Water: medium

Problems: none specific

Native: Eastern United States

Range: Zones 3 to 9

Remarks: can be used as clipped hedge

is larger than summersweet and has fragrant white flowers.

Sweet Bay Magnolia

Magnolia virginiana

Sweet bay magnolia is best known for the shimmer of the silvery undersides of its dark green leaves. Evergreen in the coastal and lower South, sweet bay magnolia loses its leaves in the winter from the middle South northward.

This native American tree, also known as laurel or swamp magnolia, is prized for its foliage, its form, and its smooth silver-gray bark.

In the Landscape

In its native South, sweet bay magnolia can grow to a height of 40 to 60 feet. More often, in a garden landscape, the tree grows to about 25 feet with a spread of about 6 feet.

The 3-inch, cup-shaped blooms are much smaller than those of Southern magnolia (page 122) and have a pleasant lemony fragrance. They appear in May and June and sporadically throughout the summer. Later, spent blooms become cone-shaped seed pods spiked with bright red seeds.

The multitrunked form of this tree makes an excellent accent or a free-form screen. Its distinguishing leaves, with their silvery undersides, give the tree a dramatic shimmer when a breeze moves its limbs.

Planting and Care

Sweet bay magnolia tolerates sunny and shady locations. In Tennessee and Kentucky and locations farther north, it

The white flowers of sweet bay magnolia bring a lemony-sweet scent to the garden.

should be protected from freezing winter winds.

Unlike most other magnolias, sweet bay magnolia thrives in wet and swampy soil, and prefers the same conditions in the garden.

Species and Selections

Although few named selections exist, there are many natural selections with different forms and leaf patterns. Recommended selections include 'Havener', which produces double flowers, and 'Opelousas', whose flowers and leaves are unusually large. 'Henry Hicks' is a hardy evergreen selection that remains green at temperatures well below zero degrees Fahrenheit.

AT A GLANCE

Plant type: semievergreen tree

Features: dark green foliage with silvery undersides, lemon-scented blooms

Colors: creamy white flowers

Height: 40 to 60 feet

Light: full sun to partial shade

Soil: organic

Water: medium

Problems: none specific

Native: Eastern United States

Range: Zones 5 to 9

Remarks: evergreen in Southern range

Sweetshrub

Calycanthus floridus

When the flowers of sweetshrub appear in spring, the blooms emit a delightful fruity fragrance. The flowers of this old-fashioned shrub smell so sweet that they are often used in sachets. The shiny leaves are also aromatic when crushed, and turn a cheerful yellow in the fall.

This deciduous shrub is native to the Southeastern United States from Virginia to Florida.

In the Landscape

Sweetshrub has an irregular growth habit in the wild, reaching 6 to 9 feet in height and 6 to 15 feet in width. Given proper growing conditions, sweetshrub takes on a dense, rounded form.

This shrub's most notable asset is its unusual-looking reddish brown flowers, which appear in April and May. When warmed by the sunlight on humid, spring days, the fragrance is intoxicating.

Sweetshrub is a versatile plant that mixes well with other shrubs in the landscape. Plant it near a patio or entrance where the aroma can be enjoyed. To enjoy its fragrance, cut a few branches of the shrub and use them in floral arrangements.

Planting and Care

Sweetshrub adapts to a wide variety of horticultural conditions. It will grow in shade as well as full sun. In shaded

The foliage of sweetshrub turns a vibrant yellow in the fall (above). Fragrant reddish brown flowers bloom in April and May (right).

locations, the form is irregular, yet graceful. In full sun, its growth habit is more compact and dense. Although it will grow in almost any soil, for ideal growth, provide moist, organic soil. If plants become overgrown, prune them after flowering in the spring.

Species and Selections

Several named selections have been bred for their fragrance and flower color. 'Athens' is known for its cantaloupe-scented yellow flowers. Other selections include 'Edith Wilder' and 'Urbana', which have deep brown-maroon flowers and a sweet fragrance. 'Purpureus' has purple leaves.

AT A GLANCE

Plant type: deciduous shrub

Features: fragrant blooms with ribbonlike petals, dark green aromatic leaves that turn yellow in fall, urn-shaped fruit

Colors: reddish brown flowers

Height: 6 to 9 feet

Light: full sun to deep shade

Soil: moist, organic

Water: medium

Problems: none specific

Native: Southeastern United States

Range: Zones 4 to 9

Remarks: grows in almost any soil

Tartarian Aster

Aster tataricus

Tartarian aster brings texture, color, and height to the flower garden in late fall. The plant is distinguished by 2-foot-long leaves and profuse spikes of pale blue-purple flowers that top 9-foot stems.

A dependable perennial that thrives in sandy or heavy soil, Tartarian aster is native to Siberia.

In the Landscape

Like many other fall-blooming perennials, this plant has a vigorous growth habit. Tartarian aster looks good at the back of a flower border where its tall stature can be appreciated.

Pair this perennial with other late-blooming plants, including tall ornamental grasses, mums, white boltonia (page 146), and marigolds.

Tartarian aster is one of the last perennials to bloom, often flowering as late as November while still maintaining a fresh look. As the nights get cooler, flower colors intensify.

Planting and Care

Because of its tall, lanky character, this plant requires staking. To produce sturdier plants, pinch them in late spring and early summer.

Tartarian aster prefers full sun and well-drained, moderately fertile soil. To propagate and rejuvenate the plants, divide them routinely every few years in the early spring or fall.

The lanky stems of tartarian aster rest on stonecrop (above). The height of this aster works beautifully in the back of a perennial border (right).

Species and Selections

Very few selections exist, but the straight species is readily available from nurseries. 'Jindai' is a low-growing form that grows only 4 feet tall and is less likely to need staking than other asters. Related species include New England aster, *A. novae-angliae* (page 104), Frikart's aster, *A. x frikartii*, and New York aster or Michaelmas daisy, *A. novibelgii.* Bigleaf aster, *A. macrophyllus,* another fall-blooming species, is native to the Eastern United States and bears heart-shaped leaves and violet, lavender, or light blue flowers.

AT A GLANCE

Plant type: perennial

Features: daisylike fall blooms

Colors: blue to lavender

Height: 3 to 9 feet

Light: full sun

Soil: well drained, moderately fertile

Water: medium during summer

Problems: none specific

Native: Siberia

Range: Zones 4 to 8

Remarks: striking plant for the back of a border

Threadleaf Coreopsis

Coreopsis verticillata

Threadleaf coreopsis is probably the toughest and most drought tolerant of all species of coreopsis. Named for its fernlike, finely dissected foliage, this plant spreads underground to form ever-widening clumps and sports bright yellow blooms all summer long. This perennial is native from Maryland to Florida and west to Arkansas.

In the Landscape

Threadleaf coreopsis grows to a height of 18 inches to 2 feet and is a natural choice for the middle of the border. Individual plants grow broadly and in mounds. Depending on the selection, flower color ranges from pale lemon yellow to golden yellow. With its fine, fernlike leaves, threadleaf coreopsis is a good companion to plants with more coarsely textured foliage.

Planting and Care

Threadleaf coreopsis prefers soil that is poor but well-drained. For best flowering, plant this perennial in full sun, although many selections grow successfully with light afternoon shade. Arrange the plants in groups of three or more at the edge of woodland areas or in a meadow. Although the blooming season occurs in summer, a light shearing may encourage repeat blooming in the fall.

To rejuvenate the planting, divide threadleaf coreopsis every year or two in fall or early spring.

The needlelike leaves of coreopsis offer an attractive backdrop for its bright yellow flowers.

Species and Selections

Although this species is a popular garden perennial, many selections are available in garden centers.

'Golden Showers', a larger selection, bears 18-inch to 2-foot mounds of buttercup yellow blossoms. 'Moonbeam', a 1992 Perennial Plant of the Year, has pale yellow flowers and requires little to no deadheading. A good dwarf form is 'Zagreb', an 18-inch tall plant that grows in a compact habit and bears deep yellow flowers.

AT A GLANCE

Plant type: perennial

Features: fine foliage, daisy-like flowers from spring until fall

Colors: pale to golden yellow flowers

Height: 2 to 3 feet

Light: full sun

Soil: poor, well drained

Water: low

Problems: none specific

Native: Southeastern United States

Range: Zones 3 to 9

Remarks: easy to grow, heat tolerant

Two-winged Silverbell
Halesia diptera

When two-winged silverbell bursts into bloom in early spring, it gives the appearance of snowflakes falling. Also known as snowdrop tree, this plant is covered in delicate white bell-shaped blooms. Native to the woodlands of the Southeastern United States, this species is underutilized simply because it is not widely available.

In the Landscape

At maturity, two-winged silverbell can reach a height of 20 to 30 feet with a 10 foot spread. It grows in a multistemmed, rounded habit. In wooded locations, this attractive small tree tends to take on a more irregular growth habit. Place two-winged silverbell where its graceful, bell-shaped flowers can be viewed, perhaps beside a deck or a patio. The tree's blooms are also a favorite of hummingbirds.

Two-winged silverbell gets its common name from the shape of its fruit, which has distinctly shaped "wings." When green, the fruit has a sour lemon-lime flavor.

Planting and Care

Because two-winged silverbell is an understory tree in nature, it prefers a partially shady location. However, it will tolerate full sun if provided well-drained, moist, fertile, slightly acidic soil. Flowers are sparse when grown in full shade.

This species can't tolerate drought, so water it during dry periods in summer. Feed the

The bell-shaped white flower clusters of two-winged silverbell hang gracefully from its branches.

tree in late winter with an all-purpose fertilizer.

Species and Selections

'Magniflora' is a selection with larger flowers than the species and is dramatic when in full bloom. Carolina silverbell, *H. carolina*, is a related species native to the Southeastern United States. This plant is more widely available in nurseries because it flowers heavily and grows larger than two-winged silverbell. Another species that grows in the mountains of North Carolina, Tennessee, and Georgia is mountain silverbell, *H. monticola*. This is the tallest-growing tree of the species, reaching a height of 60 feet and bearing larger flowers.

AT A GLANCE

Plant type: deciduous tree

Features: bell-shaped spring blooms, multistemmed growth habit

Colors: white flower clusters

Height: 20 to 30 feet

Light: partial shade, tolerates full sun with moisture

Soil: well drained, moist, fertile, slightly acidic

Water: medium

Problems: none specific

Native: Southeastern United States

Range: Zones 5 to 8

Remarks: plant where its blooms will be shown to advantage, intolerant of drought

Variegated Solomon's-seal

Polygonatum odoratum 'Variegatum'

Variegated Solomon's-seal is an elegant, native plant best known for the distinct creamy white edging on its foliage. The leaves, combined with its delicate, bell-shaped blooms, bring a refined look to shady summer gardens. If it's not too hot or dry, this wildflower will grow almost anywhere in the United States.

In the Landscape

This perennial blooms in late spring with inch-long, greenish white flowers that dangle like bells from its arching stems. On spring evenings, the flowers emit a lilylike scent. After flowering, blue-black berries appear in fall, and the leaves turn a golden brown.

Variegated Solomon's-seal is a versatile landscape plant that is attractive in many settings. It works well as part of a shaded border or in a wildflower garden. It also makes a good companion for other shade-loving plants, especially those with a finer texture, such as ferns and astilbes. The striking foliage also lends itself to floral arrangements.

Planting and Care

This species is native to cool, moist sites, so for best growth, provide rich, moist, organic soil and partial to full shade. Variegated Solomon's-seal spreads by underground rhizomes, producing large clumps in a short amount of time. Propagate this perennial by dividing the rhizomes with a knife in the spring.

Plant variegated Solomon's-seal in the shade of a tree for extra greenery and texture (above). Pairs of bell-shaped flowers surrounded by striped foliage dangle from the stems (right).

Species and Selections

Great Solomon's-seal (*P. commutatum),* a related plant, is coarser than the species and generally grows taller, reaching a height of 3 to 5 feet.

Another native species is small Solomon's-seal (*P. biflorum),* a plant with yellowish white tubular-shaped flowers that grows only 2 to 3 feet tall. False Solomon's-seal (*Smilacina racemosa*) is a perennial with small white flowers that grow in pyramid-shaped clusters. The blooms are followed by small, whitish berries that turn red in autumn.

AT A GLANCE

Plant type: perennial

Features: variegated, arching foliage; small, drooping flowers; grapelike berries in fall

Colors: creamy white flowers

Height: 2 to 3 feet

Light: partial to full shade

Soil: moist, organic

Water: low to medium

Problems: none specific

Native: North America

Range: Zones 3 to 9

Remarks: foliage has fall color

Virginia Sweetspire

Itea virginica

Although native to the Eastern United States, in the past, Virginia sweetspire was not often found in Southern gardens. Today it is available from many special-ity nurseries and catalogs. With its fragrant white flower spikes, graceful character, and beautiful fall color, this shrub provides a natural screen.

In the Landscape

Virginia sweetspire grows to a height of 3 to 9 feet with an equal spread. Blooming when few trees and shrubs do, it has dense 2- to 5-inch spikes of fragrant white flowers that appear in late spring and con-tinue until summer.

Virginia sweetspire is well suited for a natural landscape or a mixed perennial border. Even though this shrub is evergreen to semievergreen in most climates, the leaves turn scarlet to maroon in the fall, often remaining on the plant until December.

Planting and Care

In its native habitat, Virginia sweetspire is found growing along streams, so it flourishes in moist soil. It prefers fertile, organic soil and will mature rapidly with adequate mois-ture and nutrition. This shrub grows well in either full sun or partial shade, although its form will be more compact and dense if grown in full sun.

Regular pruning is not nec-essary, but, it's a good idea to remove old stems to allow more light and space for new

Be sure to give Virginia sweet-spire lots of room—it grows as wide as it does tall (right). The shrub's leaves turn brilliant colors in fall (above).

growth. Propagation is by simple division.

Species and Selections

There are few selections of this species, although you will find plants that vary in flower and leaf color. 'Henry's Garnet' is a 3- to 5-foot tall plant with vivid garnet red fall color and blooms larger than those of Virginia sweetspire. 'Saturnalia' is more compact than the species, but it has the same fragrant white summer flowers. An added bonus is its fall color, which ranges from yellow to orange to red and is superior to that of the species.

AT A GLANCE

Plant type: evergreen shrub

Features: late-spring to early-summer fragrant blooms, brilliant red fall color

Colors: white flowers

Height: 3 to 9 feet

Light: full sun to partial shade

Soil: fertile, organic, moist

Water: medium

Problems: none specific

Native: Eastern United States

Range: Zones 5 to 9

Remarks: available from specialty nursery catalogs

White Boltonia

Boltonia asteroides

White boltonia blooms from late summer to early fall, providing an extended display of white, daisylike flowers. A native American wildflower, white boltonia is a carefree garden perennial that grows from New York to North Dakota and south to Florida and Texas.

In the Landscape

This plant has a wide-spreading growth habit, so it is best to plant it toward the rear of a flower border. It can reach a flowering height of 3 to 6 feet, with a spread of 3 to 4 feet. Its neutral color and graceful form combine easily with other fall-blooming perennials, including asters (pages 104 and 136), ironweed, Russian sage (page 114), and ornamental grasses.

Planting and Care

Plant white boltonia in full sun, providing it with fertile, well-drained, soil rich in organic matter. Since this species grows rapidly in one season, allow plenty of space for its wide-spreading character. If necessary, divide the clumps in the spring.

Species and Selections

The selection 'Snowbank' is preferred over the species because of its neat, compact growth habit. It only grows 3 feet tall and doesn't require staking when grown in full sun. For color variety, 'Pink Beauty' bears pale pink flowers and has a compact growth habit. These two plants grow quickly,

Fresh as daisies, the flowers of white boltonia (above) virtually cover the plant in summer. 'Snowbank' is popular because it grows in a compact manner (right).

reaching a height of 3 to 4 feet in just one growing season. Because of their strong stems, they require little to no staking. The species is easily grown from seed, but both of these selections must be propagated by division.

Other species with ornamental value are Japanese boltonia (*B. indica*), which has double white flowers, and violet boltonia (*B. asteroides latisquama*), a North American native with pink to purple flowers.

AT A GLANCE

Plant type: perennial

Features: daisylike late-summer flowers

Colors: white blooms

Height: 3 to 6 feet

Light: full sun

Soil: well drained, fertile

Water: medium during summer

Problems: none specific

Native: United States

Range: Zones 4 to 9

Remarks: carefree perennial

White Oak

Quercus alba

The majestic white oak is a prized specimen shade tree. It grows from a pyramidal form when young, into a broad, rounded tree that may exceed 90 feet in height with a 50- to 80-foot spread. The leaves of white oak are 5 to 9 inches long and about 4 inches wide, turning brilliant colors in autumn.

Native from Maine to Northern Florida and west to Minnesota and Texas, this oak is a source of lumber for furniture, flooring, and wine and whiskey barrels. Its acorns are a source of food for wild turkey and squirrels.

In the Landscape

White oak grows slowly, sometimes taking 60 years to achieve its full height and spread. When given enough room to grow and mature, it acquires an upright, rounded form.

In spring, light gray, pink-tinted foliage appears and turns dark green in summer. Fall color is later than other deciduous species, with the leaves turning spectacular shades of red to reddish purple.

With age, the tree's bark breaks into whitish gray vertical plates that have a wintery appearance.

White oak makes a good street tree, even where electrical and telephone wires may be present. Its open growth habit allows wires to pass through the crown with a minimum of interference from branches.

The leaves of the majestic white oak have rounded lobes and turn brilliant shades of red to purple in fall.

Planting and Care

White oak is difficult to transplant. The best chances for success in the home landscape come from planting young 3- to 5-foot-tall, container-grown trees. If you want to transplant a large tree, it will be worth your while to turn the task over to landscape professionals.

Plant white oak in full sun and rich, slightly acidic soil. During periods of drought, be sure to give it plenty of water. In natural areas, allow the fallen leaves to decay in the tree's feeding area to replenish organic matter and nutrients, and to maintain soil acidity. Prune the branches in winter or early spring before new growth appears.

AT A GLANCE

Plant type: deciduous tree

Features: large, spreading form; plated bark, red fall color

Height: 70 to 90 feet

Light: full sun to partial shade

Soil: well drained, moist, fertile, acidic

Water: medium

Problems: none specific

Native: Eastern United States

Range: Zones 3 to 9

Remarks: good choice for street plantings

Species and Selections

Other oaks that grow successfully are Shumard oak (*Q. shumardii*), willow oak (*Q. phellos*), and overcup oak (*Q. lyrata*).

Winter Daphne

Daphne odora

Although fragrance in the garden is usually associated with spring, there are many plants that scent the landscape in winter. One of these is winter daphne, an evergreen shrub that is an old-fashioned favorite.

While this plant was popular in the early 1900s, today's gardeners often overlook winter daphne in favor of easier-to-grow plants. But in the lower South, the plant has always been prized for its extraordinarily fragrant small flowers. Some gardeners even consider it sweeter than the gardenia.

In the Landscape

Winter daphne is a dwarf evergreen shrub that grows slowly to a height of 4 feet. At maturity, it has a mounded, slightly irregular form. Its foliage is glossy green and many selections have variegated leaves. This shrub's waxy, nosegaylike flowers appear in late winter and last about four weeks.

Even before the first blossoms open, the buds put on a show. The pink-flowered selections will remain in pointed clusters for weeks until a few warm days in late winter coax them into bloom.

Planting and Care

Winter daphne is finicky about soil conditions and can be difficult to grow. It needs well-drained, fertile soil, but it can adapt to either alkaline or acidic soil.

Plant winter daphne in a

As a foundation planting (right), the delectable scent of winter daphne permeates a porch. The species 'Aureo-marginata' has pink rosettes that contrast with its glossy green leaves (above).

location where its fragrance can be appreciated. The site must receive partial shade, however, because direct sunlight will burn the foliage.

After the initial watering, this shrub requires little attention.

Species and Selections

The selection 'Alba' has creamy white flowers, while 'Aureo-marginata' has leaves bordered with yellow. 'Variegata' has leaves with pronounced yellow margins and pale pink flowers.

A popular hybrid among Southern gardeners is burkwood daphne, *D.* x *burkwoodii*). For delicate, light pink

AT A GLANCE

Plant type: evergreen shrub

Features: fragrant winter blooms, variegated leaves

Colors: white to pink flowers

Height: 4 feet

Light: partial to full shade

Soil: well drained, fertile

Water: light

Problems: none specific

Native: China, Japan

Range: Zones 7 to 9

Remarks: intolerant of overwatering

flowers, choose 'Carol Mackie'. There are many selections of the low-growing rose or garland daphne, *D. cneorum*, that are just as fragrant as winter daphne.

Winterberry

Ilex verticillata

Winterberry is a member of the holly family, one of the most varied and useful groups of Southern American landscape plants. Although many hollies are evergreen, winterberry is a deciduous shrub. Losing its leaves, however, is an advantage for this tree, for that is when the bright red berries appear. Winterberry grows from as far north as Michigan and Wisconsin south to Florida and as far west as Missouri.

In the Landscape

At maturity, winterberry grows to a height of 6 to 10 feet with a similar spread. With selective pruning, this shrub can take the form of a small tree.

Winterberry's foliage is medium green, but the real color occurs from the brilliant red berries that ripen in late August and last well into winter. In the fall, the foliage turns a dark, almost black color before dropping. In some years, the leaves turn bright yellow.

Planting and Care

Winterberry grows naturally in swampy environments, thriving in heavy, poorly drained soil and in wet woodlands. For maximum fruiting, plant winterberry in full sun or partial shade.

Like all hollies, male and female winterberry plants are separate. Since most of the selections are bred for their fruiting ability, a pollinator, or

When winterberry drops its leaves in the fall, bright red berries remain on its gray stems throughout winter.

male plant, must be present for fruiting to occur.

Species and Selections

The selection 'Afterglow' has orange to orange-red fruits, while the berries of 'Fairfax' are bright red. 'Sunset' produces a heavy crop of red fruit, while 'Winter Gold' yields pinkish red fruit. 'Winter Red' is one of the best selections, with abundant bright red berries.

Hybrids with *I. serrata* include 'Apollo', a male pollinator for 'Sparkleberry'. This female selection has bright orange-red fruit that grows 8- to 10- foot tall. 'Autumn Glow' forms a compact 6- to 8- foot bush with red fruits and autumn color. 'Harvest Red'

AT A GLANCE

Plant type: deciduous shrub

Features: long-lasting, red winter berries; medium green foliage

Colors: orange-red to bright red berries

Height: 6 to 10 feet

Light: full sun to partial shade

Soil: wide range of soil conditions

Water: medium

Problems: none specific

Native: Eastern United States

Range: Zones 3 to 9

Remarks: male plant must be present for female to produce fruit

has lustrous, dark green summer foliage that turns reddish purple in fall and deep red fruit.

Woodland Phlox

Phlox divaricata

With its showy clusters of flowers and ease of care, woodland phlox is one of the best early spring-flowering perennials. This native offers striking lavender-blue flowers and a loose, informal appearance that spruces up perennial borders and brings life to shady beds and wildflower gardens.

In the Landscape

This woodland species blooms in late spring to early summer, producing pale blue flowers that have a light fragrance. Use woodland phlox in the front of a shaded border or to edge a woodland walkway.

The various blue shades of this plant are strong enough to hold their own with bolder colors, so try combining it with hyacinths or pansies.

Planting and Care

The best time to plant woodland phlox is in the fall, allowing plants time to become established before the blooming season in early spring. This plant prefers moist, organic soil and partial to full shade. Because woodland phlox has shallow roots, it's a good idea to mulch with additional organic matter to help conserve moisture. This species spreads rapidly, so clumps should be divided just after flowering, or firm, leafy stem cuttings can be taken in summer. Phlox can be sown from seed in midsummer.

Powdery mildew is sometimes a problem with this

The spreading stems of woodland phlox dapple the spring garden with a soothing blue.

species, especially with plants that have been stressed during a dry winter; however, the plant usually recovers on its own.

Species and Selections

'Dirigo Ice' is a pale lavender blue selection about 8 to 12 inches tall, while 'Chattahoochee' has lavender blue flowers with dark purple centers. Breeders have also developed a selection called 'Fuller's White' that is more sun-tolerant.

Creeping phlox (*P. stolonifera*), while not as showy or vigorous as woodland phlox, tolerates even deeper shade and is a good choice for heavily wooded landscapes.

The most common native phlox is garden phlox, *P. paniculata*. Blooming from late July until September, this perennial is available in a variety of colors.

AT A GLANCE

Plant type: perennial

Features: spring and summer blooms; low, mat-forming habit

Colors: clear blue flowers

Height: 12 to 15 inches

Light: partial to full shade

Soil: moist, organic

Water: low to medium

Problems: powdery mildew

Native: Eastern United States and west to East Texas

Range: Zones 3 to 9

Remarks: spreads quickly

Wormwood

Artemisia 'Powis Castle'

Powis Castle wormwood took the gardening world by storm when it was introduced in the late eighteenth century in Wales. Grown for its feathery gray-green foliage rather than its flowers, wormwood blends hardiness with beauty and combines with many plants in a summer flower border. With more than 200 species and selections in the artemisia family available, these plants are often grown as perennials or herbaceous herbs, since many are thought to have medicinal properties or act as insect repellents.

In the Landscape

This plant is known for its speedy growth. It can reach a height and width of 2 to 3 feet in just one growing season. To tell the difference between wormwood and other gray-leafed plants, crush the leaves and smell them. Wormwood's leaves are highly aromatic. This perennial serves as a good foil for dark-foliaged plants, providing a visual barrier between other plants with vividly contrasting flowers.

Planting and Care

Although wormwood will grow in poor, dry soil, for best results, this perennial prefers full sun and well-drained, non-organic soil.

This plant suffers in areas with high summer humidity, which can cause dieback. To rejuvenate the plant, prune dead areas. Several other species of artemisia suffer

Wormwood brings a cool feel to the summer flower border with its filigree of silver foliage.

from dieback when grown under the same conditions. To keep wormwood from becoming overgrown, prune it in either late spring or early summer.

Species and Selections

Related species of wormwood are popular landscape plants. 'Silver King' (*A. ludoviciana*) grows 3 feet tall and has silver-gray foliage. For a good dwarf form that grows only 8 to 12 inches high, choose 'Silver Mound' artemisia (*A. schmidtiana* 'Nana'). Its finely cut silver foliage grows in a silky cushionlike habit with small, drooping yellow flowers.

Southernwood (*A. abrotanum*) has aromatic foliage that was used historically to scent stored linens and to repel insects. Selections of this plant

have tangerine-, lemon-, and camphor-scented fragrances. A related species, common wormwood (*A. absintheum*), was once a source of absinthe.

Plant Problems

You will notice that many plants profiled in this book have no specific diseases or insect problems associated with them. From the inception of this book, AHS members felt it was important to choose disease- and insect-resistant plants. Plants native to the United States have evolved under conditions where survival is not an issue. But many plant problems, including low resistance to pests and diseases, result from poor care. Plants need appropriate soil, good drainage, adequate nutrition, and proper light to remain healthy.

Because of an increasing concern for the safety of our environment, the first line of defense for most plant pests should be to remove the diseased foliage. Insecticidal soaps and dormant sprays are next. If mild insecticides don't work, consult your county Extension office or local nursery for a recommendation. It often helps to bring a sample of the infested plant to identify the problem.

Diseases

Anthracnose is a common plant fungus that causes spots on leaves and lesions on twigs and fruits during wet seasons. Flowering dogwood is particularly susceptible. Completely remove affected foliage and destroy dead wood in the tree and leaves on the ground yearly. Check with your local Extension service before applying any fungicide registered for prevention or control of anthracnose.

Fire blight is a bacterial disease, and the name describes its early symptoms. Branches look reddish brown, as if on fire, and they later turn black and die. If left untreated, it often kills a plant. Members of the rose family, including loquat, are susceptible to this disease. To control it, spray the plants while they are in bloom, since fire blight is carried by bees. Prune diseased sections; between cuts, dip pruning shears in a weak bleach solution to disinfect shears. The most effective method of prevention is to select varieties that are resistant to fire blight.

Leaf spots are small, discolored blotches on leaves. Sometimes they can be serious enough to result in defoliation. To control the problem, follow the recommendations of your local nursery or county agent. As a last resort, use copper sprays.

Powdery mildew is an affliction that is usually more unsightly than lethal. It looks like white to gray mildew and appears on the upper leaf surfaces of the affected plant. It is most evident during cool, humid weather, particularly in the spring and fall. With the most serious infestations, the leaves become dry and wither, and the plant can die. Use preventative sprays on species prone to this disease, such as crepe myrtle, flowering dogwood, and oak. Good air circulation around plants can also minimize the damage.

Insects

Aphids are tiny pear-shaped insects that suck sap from tender young leaves, stems, or flower buds. As a result, the plant's growth is distorted and buds will not open. These

Anthracnose

Fire blight

Powdery mildew

insects produce a liquid honeydew, which often serves as a growing medium for sooty mold. This condition, while not attractive, will not damage a tree and will disappear once the insects are controlled. Aphids particularly like crepe myrtle and river birch, although they will feed on other species. These insects produce hundreds of offspring in a few weeks, so early control is crucial. Spray infected foliage with dormant oils or insecticides.

Japanese beetles chew on foliage, often completely defoliating many garden perennials. Control is sometimes difficult, since grubs, the immature form of the beetles, are found in lawns. Minimize adult populations by treating large areas of turf with pesticides.

Lacebugs are flat insects with lacy wings that feed on the undersides of leaves, causing them to dry up and fall. A telltale sign of lacebug damage is tiny black spots of excrement on the undersides of leaves. Lacebugs are most severe in late summer or early fall and can be eliminated by spraying with insecticides.

Leaf miners are tiny larvae that tunnel and feed between the upper and lower surfaces of a leaf, leaving blisters and serpentine trails or "mines" that disfigure the leaf. Leaf miners are generally the young of flies, beetles, sawflies, or moths, and will appear as small, oblong larvae at the fresh end of a mine. Many shrubs can tolerate feeding by leaf miners without serious damage. However, if the pests are eating more than one-third of the leaf's surface, spray the shrub with a systemic pesticide. Azaleas are particularly susceptible.

Mealybugs are cottonlike insects ¼ inch long that suck sap from leaves and stems, causing deformed foliage. Use oil sprays or insecticidal soaps to control them.

Scales are soft- or hard-bodied insects that cling to the underside of leaves and along stems, drinking nectar from the tree. The hard-bodied types look like tiny raised surfaces on the leaf or stem and can be scraped away with a fingernail. Soft-bodied types may be covered in white wax or a mass of cottonlike fibers. While many trees are susceptible to scales, Canadian hemlock is particularly vulnerable. To control scales, spray the eggs in winter with dormant oils. These pests are more difficult to kill when they are older. The eggs are naturally resistant to pesticides, so a second dose is often necessary to kill young scales as they emerge.

Spider mites drink nectar from the undersides of leaves, flower buds, and young stems. These microscopic insects are worst in spring and fall, especially during dry weather. You may not see spider mites until their feeding makes the tops of the leaves look faded and mottled. Turning over an infested leaf reveals clusters of pinpoint-sized spider mites and their delicate webbing. To control these pests, thoroughly coat the underside of the leaves with pesticide. Sometimes mites disappear on their own when the temperature climbs to 90 degrees or higher.

Webworms appear as large webs spun over twigs and branches in late summer or early fall. The webs contain caterpillars that devour the foliage. To control them, prune damaged sections and destroy the webs. If serious infestations occur, thoroughly cover the webs with a pesticide.

Aphids

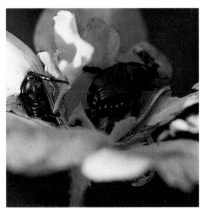

Japanese beetles

Spider mites

Glossary

Alleé: A path lined with trees.

Balled-and-burlapped plant: A tree or shrub dug from a field with a ball of soil around the roots; the root ball is held together with burlap.

Bare-root plant: One that has its bare roots exposed.

Bracts: Modified leaves associated with flowers, especially on dogwoods.

Branch structure: The manner in which a plant's branches grow; can be spreading or upright, orderly or erratic.

Character: The manner in which a plant grows.

Cold hardy: Able to survive in below-freezing temperatures.

Container-grown plant: A plant grown from seed in a container or pot.

Crown: A tree or shrub's head of foliage.

Deciduous: Having leaves that shed in fall.

Dieback: Death of the tip shoots of plants as a result of abnormal heat, cold, drought, fungus, or insect infestation.

Dioecious: Having male reproductive organs on one plant and female on another.

Espalier: A plant trained to grow against a support.

Foundation plants: Shrubs planted at the base of a building.

Ground cover: Low-growing plants that spread to cover the ground.

Growth habit: The manner in which a plant grows.

Herbaceous: Having no persistent woody stem above ground.

Hybrid: An offspring of two plants of different species or varieties.

Knees: An abrupt bend or outgrowth in a stem or tree trunk.

Lobe: A curved or rounded projection or division on a leaf.

Ornamental: A plant grown for its beauty and character.

Panicle: A pyramidal, loosely branched flower cluster.

Persistent: Continuing without change instead of falling, whether dead or live.

Pollinator: A male plant that pollinates female plants.

Propagate: To increase by sexual or asexual reproduction.

Prune: To remove dead, broken, or diseased branches.

Reflexed: Leaves or stems that turn abruptly downward.

Rhizome: An underground stem enlarged by food storage.

Selection: Seedlings with more desirable characteristics than others.

Self-sowing plant: One that sows itself by dropping seeds.

Softwood cutting: A cutting that is taken from new wood.

Species: A group of plants that has characteristics that distinguishes it from other groups.

Specimen plant: An individual plant that is effective when planted alone.

Stamen: The pollen-bearing male organ of a flower.

Sucker: A shoot that sprouts from the roots or from beneath the ground.

Taproot: An unusually long main root that usually grows straight down.

Understory tree: A tree that thrives in the shadow of a larger tree.

Upright tree: One that provides little shade because of its straight up-and-down growth.

Woody: Having the texture of a tree.

Bibliography

Armitage, Allan M. *Herbaceous Perennial Plants: A Treatise on Their Identification, Culture, and Garden Attributes.* Athens: Varsity Press, Inc. 1989.

Bales, Suzanne Frutig. *Perennials. Burpee American Gardening Series.* New York: Prentice Hall Press, 1991.

Bir, Richard E. *Growing and Propagating Showy Native Woody Plants.* Chapel Hill: The University of North Carolina Press, 1992.

Dirr, Michael A. *Manual of Woody Landscape Plants: Their Identification, Ornamental Characteristics, Culture, Propagation, and Uses.* Champaign: Stipes Publishing Company, 1990.

Glasener, Erica, and Walter Reeves. *Georgia Gardener's Guide.* Franklin: Cool Spring Press, 1997.

Jones, Samuel B., and Leonard E. Foote. *Gardening with Native Wildflowers.* Portland: Timber Press, 1990.

Poor, Janet M., and Nancy P. Brewster. *Plants that Merit Attention, Vol. II—Shrubs.* Portland: Timber Press, 1996.

Poor, Janet M. *Plants that Merit Attention, Vol. I Trees.* Portland: Timber Press, 1984.

Southern Living magazine garden staff. *Trees & Shrubs.* Birmingham: Oxmoor House, 1980.

Still, Steven M. *Manual of Herbaceous Ornamental Plants.* Champaign: Stipes Publishing Company, 1994.

Watkins, John V., and Thomas J. Sheehan. *Florida Landscape Plants.* Gainesville: The University of Florida Press, 1976.

Welch, William C. *Perennial Garden Color for Texas and the South.* Dallas: Taylor Publishing Company, 1989.